Keith Payne is a professor of psychology and neuroscience at the University of North Carolina at Chapel Hill. As an international leader in the psychology of inequality and discrimination his research has been featured in *The Atlantic*, the *New York Times* and on NPR, and he has written for *Scientific American* and *Psychology Today*.

Praise for *The Broken Ladder*

'Brilliant ... an important, fascinating read ... Payne challenges a common perception that the real problem isn't inequality but poverty, and he's persuasive that societies are shaped not just by disadvantage at the bottom but also by inequality across the spectrum'

Nicholas Kristof, *New York Times*

'Authoritative, thought-provoking, accessible and well worth a spot on your summer reading list ... Payne embraces the egalitarian view that inequality of income is problem in and of itself ... While we have come to understand that a society can suffer from having either too much inequality or too little, the challenge now is identifying and getting to that sweet spot in between'

Steven Pearlstein, *Washington Post*

'Keith Payne is intent on showing how the problem of inequality operates within the human mind ... Beyond its case studies, the memoir portion of Payne's book is compelling in its own way, and is a counter-narrative to J. D. Vance's *Hillbilly Elegy* ... Payne's book will make its readers pause to consider the human condition in more depth' Nancy Isenberg, *The American Scholar*

'Sobering stuff ... [I]t should make us think about the hidden costs of growing income inequality – and about the messages society is sending to people about where they fit in'

The National Book Review

'Compelling ... [A]n engaging interdisciplinary blend of psychology, sociology and economics that will also appeal to avid readers of politics'   *Booklist*

'Keith Payne has written an eye-opening book with profound resonance for the state of our world. We all know that income inequality has dire economic and societal consequences, but *The Broken Ladder* shows that it has deep psychological impact too, affecting our decision-making, our mood and our health. A thoughtful look – and a rallying cry – into the way our environment shapes us all'   Susan Cain, author of *Quiet*

'*The Broken Ladder*'s examination of the consequences of inequality – of what it is like to be poor and to feel poor – is as profound as it is revelatory. Keith Payne is a lovely, graceful writer. Replete with gems of research studies, insights and illuminating examples and implications, this book will change the way you think about your world'   Sonja Lyubomirsky, author of *The How of Happiness*

'*The Broken Ladder* is an important, timely and beautifully written account of how inequality affects us all. Though it surely plagues the poorest and most vulnerable members of society, Keith Payne expertly and engagingly shows that it also touches the wealthy and privileged. Payne marshals the cutting edge in psychology and neuroscience research to explain how inequality influences our political and religious beliefs, how we perform at work and how we respond to stress and physical threats – and how we can combat its most insidious effects on our lives'

Adam Alter, author of *Irresistible*

THE BROKEN LADDER

HOW INEQUALITY CHANGES THE WAY WE THINK, LIVE AND DIE

KEITH PAYNE

WEIDENFELD & NICOLSON

First published in Great Britain in 2017
This paperback edition first published in 2018
by Weidenfeld & Nicolson
an imprint of The Orion Publishing Group Ltd
Carmelite House, 50 Victoria Embankment
London EC4Y 0DZ

An Hachette UK Company

1 3 5 7 9 10 8 6 4 2

A CIP catalogue record for this book is
available from the British Library.

ISBN (paperback) 978 1 4746 0112 2
ISBN (ebook) 978 1 4746 0113 9

Printed in Great Britain by
CPI Group (UK) Ltd, Croydon, CR0 4YY

www.orionbooks.co.uk

For Lucy,
my reason that tomorrow has to be better than today

CONTENTS

Introduction

The flight from Washington, D.C., to Jacksonville, Florida, takes two hours, more than enough time to change a life. No one knows why Joseph Sharkey stood up on that flight, turned around, and placed the passenger seated behind him in coach in a headlock. Maybe the passenger was talking too loud. Maybe he was bumping the back of the seat with his foot. According to witnesses, the passenger did nothing to provoke the attack. The ruckus brought the flight crew scrambling to break it up. Sharkey, undeterred, kneed a flight attendant in the groin. He then walked to the emergency exit door and tried to open it in midflight. The flight attendant and several passengers finally managed to overwhelm him and placed him in plastic handcuffs. He was arrested when the plane touched down, and faced up to twenty years in prison.

Bad behavior in first class has a different flavor. In 2009 Ivana Trump was on a flight from Palm Beach to New York when some children seated nearby started making noise. She put on headphones to drown out the commotion, but then a crying baby pushed her too far. She flew into a rage, allegedly calling the children "little fuckers" as officers escorted her off the plane.

Airplanes are microcosms of our world and the everyday anxieties we encounter there. We are thrown together with hundreds of strangers, forced into a level of intimacy ordinarily reserved for loved ones or professional colleagues. We are crammed into a narrow metal tube, triggering our evolved fear of enclosed spaces. Once the plane is aloft, there is no escape, and time seems to drag on without end. We find ourselves thousands of feet in the air, triggering our evolved fear of heights. The aircraft rumbles and shakes just enough to never let us forget that we are stranded in the air with nothing, so far as we can see, holding us up. So we sit, lacking control over when we depart and when we arrive, and when we can use our approved electronic devices. We wait, unsure of who is on board with us, how well the flight is going, or who owns the armrest. All the while, we are reminded of our mortality. What experience could be more existential?

But even more than the anxieties they provoke, there is another aspect to airplanes that makes them a notable microcosm of life. Airplanes are the physical embodiment of a status hierarchy. They are a social ladder made of aluminum and upholstery in which the rungs are represented by rows, by boarding groups, and by seating classes.

Picturing the seating plan of a plane in these terms helps explain why people attack strangers and curse at children in the strange confines of the friendly skies. A recent study led by psychologists Katherine DeCelles and Michael Norton showed that the status hierarchy of air travel is a dramatic, if hidden, force on our behavior while flying. The researchers analyzed data from millions of flights to identify what factors predicted the incidence of air rage. First they compared flights that had a first-class section to those that did not. They reasoned that if status inequalities were driving bad behavior, then we should see more air rage on flights that have a first-class cabin than those that don't. As they discovered, the odds of an air rage incident were almost four times higher in the coach section of a plane with a first-class cabin than in a plane that did not have one. Other factors mattered, too, like flight delays. But the presence of a first-class section raised the chances of a disturbance by the same amount as a nine-and-a-half-hour delay.

To test the idea another way, the researchers looked at how the boarding process highlights status differences. Most planes with a first-class cabin board at the front, which forces the coach passengers to trudge down the aisle, dragging their baggage past the well-heeled and the already comfortably seated. But about 15 percent of flights board in the middle or at the back of the plane, which spares the coach passengers this gauntlet. As predicted, air rage was about twice as likely on flights that boarded at the front, raising the chances of an incident by the same amount as waiting out a six-hour delay.

This air rage study is revealing, but not just because it illustrates how inequality drives wedges between the haves and the have-nots. What makes it fascinating to me is that incidents of rage take place even when there are no true have-nots on a flight. Since an average economy-class ticket costs several hundred dollars, few genuinely poor people can afford to travel on a modern commercial airplane. Yet even relative differences among the respectable middle-class people flying coach can create conflict and chaos. In fact, the chaos is not limited to coach: First-class flyers in the study were several times more likely to erupt in air rage when they were brought up close and personal with the rabble on front-loading planes. As Ivana Trump's behavior can attest, when the level of inequality becomes too large to ignore, everyone starts acting strange.

But they do not act strange in just any old way. Inequality affects our actions and our feelings in the same systematic, predictable fashion again and again. It makes us shortsighted and prone to risky behavior, willing to sacrifice a secure future for immediate gratification. It makes us more inclined to make self-defeating decisions. It makes us believe weird things, superstitiously clinging to the world as we want it to be rather than as it is. Inequality divides us, cleaving us into camps not only of income but also of ideology and race, eroding our trust in one another. It generates stress and makes us all less healthy and less happy.

Picture a neighborhood full of people like the ones I've described above: shortsighted, irresponsible people making bad choices; mistrustful people segregated by race and by ideology; superstitious people who won't listen to reason; people who turn to self-destructive habits as they cope with the stress and anxieties of their daily lives. These are the classic tropes of poverty and could serve as a stereotypical description of the population of any poor inner-city neighborhood or depressed rural trailer park. But as we will see in the chapters ahead, inequality can produce these tendencies even among the middle class and wealthy individuals.

What is also notable about the air rage study is that it illustrates that inequality is not the same as poverty, although it can feel an awful lot like it. That phenomenon is the subject of this book. Inequality makes people *feel* poor and *act* poor, even when they're not. Inequality so mimics poverty in our minds that the United States of America, the richest and most unequal of countries, has a lot of features that better resemble a developing nation than a superpower.

As has been reported often, income and wealth inequality are higher now than they have been in generations. Today the richest eighty-five people in the world hold more wealth than the poorest 3.5 billion inhabitants of the planet combined. In America the richest 1 percent take in more than 20 percent of all income in the richest nation that has ever existed.

Comprehending the scale of economic inequality in America today is difficult because it butts up against the limits of our imagination. It's like trying to envision the distance of a light-year, or to grasp the enormity of the brain's hundred billion neurons, or how vastly greater still are the hundred trillion connections among them. Numbers like that are simply not on a human scale. So let's first look at the economy in a more relatable framework and ask how people think of their own economic positions within it.

Many human traits, like height, follow a roughly bell-shaped curve. This curve has a bulky middle, where most people are clustered around the average, with sloping tails that trail away toward zero on both ends. The pattern is the same for a wide range of traits, like the number of ridges in a fingerprint, the chemical properties of the ingredients in a Guinness, or the chest circumference of Scottish soldiers. The bell curve was once believed to be a universal law of nature. That turned out to be mistaken, but the pattern is so common that it's easy to see why earlier thinkers would have drawn that conclusion.

When people consider their own social class, they seem to think within the parameters of a bell curve. A survey by the Pew Research Center recently asked Americans to identify their class. A classic bell curve emerged, with an astounding 89 percent of respondents describing themselves as middle class. Only 7 percent viewed themselves as members of the lower class, and only 2 percent placed themselves in the upper class. In the view of Americans, we are nearly all middle class.

Look at the actual income distribution in Figure 1, however, and you will see a very different story. To put it on a human scale, I have scaled the graph so that the top one tenth of one percent is at the height of a six-foot-tall man's head. The vertical axis shows annual incomes; the horizontal axis shows how many households are at each earning level. Starting at the left of the latter, the first inch corresponds approximately to the poorest 20 percent of Americans. Progress to the top of the toe of the model's wingtips, and you reach the median income, where half of American households are below that point and half are above. The bottom 80 percent are marked off at the $100,000 point: If your family makes six

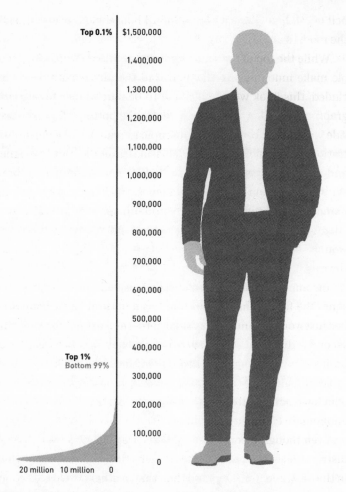

Figure 1. U.S. income distribution scaled to the height of a human.

figures, then you are in the top 20 percent, and you are four inches up the yardstick.

The big concentration on the left reveals that almost the entire population is huddled together near the bottom. The hair-thin line reaching upward shows that the number of people whose earnings reach into the millions becomes a tiny sliver. There is no bell curve here. Eighty percent of all households reside beneath the model's ankles.

While the top of the scale is capped at $1.5 million, some people make much more than that. Had the ultrawealthy been included, this book would have had to be much taller to keep the graph to scale—or the portion where the bottom 99 percent reside would have been too microscopic to read. So, like most illustrations of income distribution, this one leaves out Alex Rodriguez and most professional athletes. It does not account for Oprah Winfrey at the top of celebrity incomes, and it ignores hedge fund managers. If it did include the annual income of John Paulson, currently the highest-earning hedge fund manager, the chart would have reached not to the head of a six-foot-tall man, but to the roof of a towering building.

Income distributions are always lopsided, for two main reasons. The first is that the bottom has a natural lower boundary, because you can't make less than zero—at least not for long. The second is that it takes money to make money. Because wealth can be invested and therefore multiplied, money creates a natural cycle in which the rich get richer, stretching out the tail. Those who have nothing to invest simply can't participate in that cycle and remain clumped at the bottom.

Even though income distributions are always skewed, today's distribution in the United States is many times more unequal than in the past, and much more so than that of other developed economies. Figure 2 shows how incomes have changed over the past fifty years for each income quintile, as well as for the richest 5 percent. (The dollar amounts are adjusted for inflation.) You can see the long tail from Figure 1 in action: The rich are getting richer, while the poor are ... well, the poor are doing something interesting. The poorest fifth of Americans have been standing pretty much in place for the last fifty years.

You probably did not expect this result for the poor (or the

Figure 2. Average household income (2015 dollars), 1967–2015, by percentile. From U.S. Census.

middle class, for that matter, who have barely budged, either), as the well-known aphorism clearly states that the rich get richer while the poor get poorer. That's also the message most people gather from news headlines about America's growing inequality. We hear almost daily about growing economic anxiety, about an increasing sense of desperation and diminished hopes for the future. In one recent poll, half of Americans under thirty said the American dream was dead. That anxiety is real, and one of the aims of this book is to fully understand it. But in terms of inflation-adjusted income, the poorest fifth are right where we left them in 1967.

While the poor may not in fact be getting poorer, a striking aspect of inequality is that even standing in place feels like falling behind if other people around you are moving ahead. Have you ever been on a stationary train when a train next to you departs? It feels for all the world as if you are suddenly moving in the opposite direction. As the upper classes have become steadily richer, both the middle class and those living in poverty have felt poorer and poorer by comparison. But this feeling is not just an illusion. As we will see in the pages ahead, it has deadly serious consequences.

Shelves full of books have been written on the causes of economic inequality, focusing on such large-scale historical trends as advances in technology and globalized trade patterns, or political policies like taxation and spending priorities. This book does not deal with such analyses. Rather, it examines what inequality does to us as *people*. It investigates how the wealth of others—the top 5 percent, 1 percent, or tenth of a percent—changes how we experience the world.

Why would the wealth of the rich have an effect on how middle-class people live? After all, there is no direct logical connection between the two. There is also no logical connection between the movement of a train next to me and my own sense of motion, yet one still affects the other. The fact that it does cannot be explained by the properties of trains. Rather, the explanations can be found in the human mind, with its power to transform perceptions (*Hey, we're moving!*) into actions (*Grab the handrail!*).

Why, for example, does feeling poor subtract as many years from your life as actually being poor? Why does the size of your neighbor's house affect your stress hormones? Why does financial insecurity lead us to make self-defeating decisions that only lead to more insecurity? Why does your financial success lead you to regard those who disagree with you as idiots and morons rather than simply as people with a different opinion?

Learning the answers to these questions won't change income distribution, and *The Broken Ladder* will not offer new policy proposals to change tax rates or strengthen Social Security. It will, however, offer something just as significant. It will help explain some of the paradoxes of living in a modern, globalized, high-tech world, one where flat-screen TVs are cheap but financial security is out of reach, a world where the average house is 2,600 square feet but the family living in it cannot afford $400 cash for an emergency.

While assessing the macro-level causes and economic consequences of inequality is important, my goal here is more personal. It is to connect what we know about income distributions and census data to what it is actually like to be an individual living in this time and this place, surrounded by family and friends and coworkers all moving together into a future we don't comprehend. Understanding how wealth distributions shape our thinking can make us more adept at living within them. If enough people come to accept these ideas, they may enable us to take steps to reduce inequality itself. For now, we will begin with the human experience we recognize from turbulent planes and motionless trains and other people's elegant houses. All of which make us feel as if we are falling.

Chapter 1

Lunch Lady Economics

Why Feeling Poor Hurts Like Being Poor

I learned I was poor on the new lunch lady's first day at work. Before that, my school had had the same cashier for as long as my fourth-grade mind could remember. I knew that some kids paid when they got to the register and others, like me, didn't. But the old lunch lady passed us through the line, money or not, as smoothly as our plastic trays glided over the rail. Then one day she was gone, replaced by a younger woman who seemed to be trying hard. As I carried my food past her, she stopped me and asked for $1.25. I felt off balance, the way you do when an elevator stops too quickly. I started stammering, the only thing I could do, since I had not a cent. I would gladly have given her any amount of cash at that moment simply to escape. At that point, an older woman, tall and skinny in a pink polo shirt, like a flamingo with a hairnet, leaned over and whispered in her ear, and I was waved through. Eventually, the lunch line returned to its silent procession. But a hard week passed before the new cashier learned who paid what.

The moment when I realized what my free lunches meant is still with me, and I can feel the heat in my face as I recount it. Though my family had no less money than the day before, that moment changed everything for me. I began to notice differences between myself and my classmates. Despite the fact that we all wore the same school uniform, the kids who paid for their lunches seemed to dress better. Was it the shoes? They even had better hair. Did they go to a salon instead of having it cut with a bowl and a pair of scissors at home? We had all grown up within a dozen miles of one another, but the free-lunch kids had our parents' Southern drawls. The lunch-money kids had the generic voices of newscasters, from everywhere and nowhere at once.

Always a shy kid, I became almost completely silent at school. Who was I to speak? Suddenly a new social ladder stretched out before me, above me. Its rungs were marked with shoes and hair and accents, telegraphing a code I was just learning to decipher. It did not matter that nothing in my circumstances had changed but my perspective. Now I was, in fact, poor.

If you are used to thinking about wealth and poverty purely in financial terms, the way an accountant would, my response makes no sense. My insight did not change my parents' income. It did not change our monthly expenses. It changed nothing in the world, except for me. But by redirecting my attention and altering my perceptions, my thoughts, and my actions, it changed my future.

To understand how we think about status, take a look at the image of the ladder on the next page. Imagine that the people at the top of this ladder are the best off. They have the most money, the best education, and the highest-paying jobs. The people at the bottom are the worst off. They have the least money, the lowest levels of education, and the most menial jobs, if they have jobs at all. If you were to assess your own economic position with respect to that of other people, which of the ten rungs would you place yourself on?

This simple image is one of the most widely used measures of subjective social status. Let's call it the Status Ladder. We should be able to perfectly predict where a person would place himself on the ladder if we knew his income, level of education, and the prestige of his job.

Except we can't—and we can't even come close to doing so. It is true that, on average, people with higher incomes, more education, and more prestigious jobs do rate themselves higher on the ladder. But the effect is relatively small. In a sample of, say, a thousand people, some will rate themselves at the top, others will rate themselves at the bottom, and many will be in between. But only about 20 percent of their self-evaluation is based on income, education, and job status.

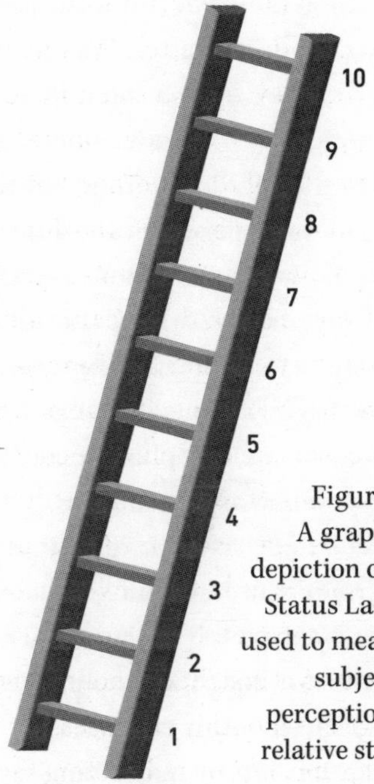

This surprisingly small relationship between traditional markers of status and

Figure 1.1. A graphical depiction of the Status Ladder, used to measure subjective perceptions of relative status.

how it is perceived subjectively means that there are a lot of people who are by objective standards affluent and yet rate themselves on the lower rungs. Similarly, many people who are objectively poor rate themselves high up the ladder.

A standard economic analysis would argue that people's own conceptions of themselves are effectively airy nothings, mere noises that flit around like the sound of static between radio stations. If subjective perceptions do not align with objectively measurable quantities like money, then so much the worse for those perceptions. Certainly, money *is* part of the story, but it's not the whole story, and not even the main character.

We have to take subjective perceptions of status seriously, because they reveal so much about people's fates. If you place yourself on a lower rung, then you are more likely in the coming years to suffer from depression, anxiety, and chronic pain. The lower the rung you select, the more probable it is that you will make bad decisions and underperform at work. The lower the rung you select, the more likely you are to believe in the supernatural and in conspiracy theories. The lower the rung you select, the more prone you are to weight issues, diabetes, and heart problems. The lower the rung you select, the fewer years you have left to live.

Let me be clear that I am not simply asserting that, if you are poor, then all of these things are more likely to happen to you. I am stating, rather, that these things are more likely to happen to you if you *feel* poor, regardless of your actual income. Of course, one reason people might feel poor is that they are actually poor. But as we have seen, that's just 20 percent of the story. For the rest of it, we have to look at ordinary middle-class people and ask why it is that, regardless of actual money, so many of them feel that they are barely getting by, that they are living paycheck to paycheck, that the neighbors know something they don't, and that if they could just earn a little more, then everything would be a little bit better. To understand the Status Ladder, we have to look beyond bank accounts and start looking at people.

All of us are aware of how much money we make, but very few of us know whether we make enough. That's because the only way we determine how much is actually "enough" is by comparing ourselves to other people. We make comparisons to other people so habitually that we rarely even notice that we are doing so. When a neighbor pulls up in a new car, we don't typically say to ourselves, "They have an Audi, so I need one, too." We are more sophisticated and mature than that. We might tell ourselves that our neighbor's good fortune is none of our business, or that she deserves the new car because of her hard work. If we do have an immediate impulse to keep pace with her, we might banish the thought as soon as it appears. And yet, the next time we get in our own car, we notice just a little more than yesterday how worn the seat is getting. Social comparison is inevitable.

It is hard to recognize such comparisons at work in our own lives, because they take place in the background, and we are experiencing the foreground. When the noise in a restaurant gets louder, for example, we begin to feel that our dinner partner is speaking quietly, because our attention is on our partner's face, not the surrounding room.

While we feel rich or poor based on the comparisons we make, the fact that social comparisons always take place in the background causes certain blind spots. Think for a minute about what matters most to you. What are the values that make you who you are? What are the motives that drive you? I have asked hundreds of people these questions over the years, and the usual responses include such ideals as love, faith, loyalty, honesty, and integrity. Although there is some variety in the answers, the whole list could be written on a business card. They are similar for men and for women, for Northerners and for Southerners, for Democrats and for Republicans. And yet, no one ever mentions something that we know to be true, both from scientific studies and from simply being human: "I crave status."

Others might not acknowledge that, but we can certainly see it in their behavior. We can observe it in the clothes they buy, in the houses they choose to live in, and in the gifts they give. Above all we can perceive it in the constantly shifting standards for what counts as "enough." If you have ever received a raise, only to adapt to the new level of income in a few months and again begin to feel as though you were still living paycheck to paycheck as before, then you can experience it in yourself. As your accomplishments rise, so do your comparison standards. Unlike the rigid columns of numbers that make up a bank ledger, status is always a moving target, because it is defined by ongoing comparisons to others.

We make social comparisons to all sorts of people on every type of occasion, yet we mysteriously manage to find ourselves on the top half of the Status Ladder again and again. We find it most comfortable to reside there. Consider for a minute how accomplished you are at your job. How intelligent are you? How moral? How loyal a friend? Are you a good driver? Deep down, you know that you are better than the average person in all these respects. In fact, the majority of people know deep down that they are better than average at most things. Which, as far as anyone can tell, is not strictly possible.

This finding is called the Lake Wobegon effect, after Garrison Keillor's fictional town "where all the women are strong, all the men are good-looking, and all the children are above average." The effect was stumbled upon in a 1965 study of accident survivors. Researchers spent six months interviewing all of the patients admitted to a Seattle hospital for injuries sustained in vehicle accidents. They compared the patients to a group of control participants who were matched on age, sex, race, and education. One of the interview questions asked the patients to rate their driving ability. Although it was not originally the main point of the study, that question is the reason that the study is remembered today, because the hospitalized patients rated themselves as better-than-average drivers. In fact, their ratings were just as high as those of the control group, who had not been in auto accidents. Clearly, these patients were not going to let the mere fact of being hospitalized after a car accident affect their self-image as good drivers.

Was it possible that the accidents were not, in fact, the patients' fault? For each case researchers examined police records to determine who was actually responsible and who was a blameless victim. After identifying those drivers who did cause the respective accidents, it was clear that their ratings were just as inflated as everyone else's.

Another early example of the effect was discovered in a massive survey by the College Board, which produces the SAT college entry exams. About a million students who took the SAT in a given year were asked to rate themselves compared with the median student (the median being the point at which half are better and half are worse). The ratings were not only about SAT performance, but also on personal characteristics like leadership and getting along with others. Seventy percent rated themselves as being above the median in leadership ability, and 85 percent rated themselves above the median in getting along well with others.

In another study, psychologist Constantine Sedikides and colleagues asked a group of volunteers to rate how good a person they were on several dimensions. The volunteers considered themselves to be more moral, kinder, more dependable, more trustworthy, and more honest than the average person—an unsurprising result, except that these volunteers were recruited by visiting a prison and enrolling convicted felons. The only category in which they did not consider themselves above average was "law abiding." Here, they rated themselves as average. Considering that they were behind bars at the time they made that judgment, it seems to lack a certain objectivity.

Over the years, hundreds of studies have replicated the Lake Wobegon effect. The studies show that most of us believe we are above average in intelligence, persistence, conscientiousness, badminton, and just about any other positive quality. The more we value the trait, the more we overrate ourselves with respect to it. My favorite study in this genre is one in which my fellow college professors were asked to rate their teaching abilities compared with those of their colleagues. A stunning 94 percent said they were better than average. One variant of this tendency is really the mother of all biases: Most people rate themselves as more objective and less biased than the average person.

Of course, pushing ourselves up the ladder in our own minds is not the only way we make the most of our social comparisons. Sometimes we pull other people down. I was recently standing in a supermarket checkout line and learned that Kim Kardashian was getting fat, Dolly Parton was wasting away, and Miley Cyrus was misusing her talent. Some housewives also seemed to be arguing with one another. Why is it that celebrity "news" showers us like confetti, but we never see headlines about Dale, the local HVAC repairman and his on-again, off-again relationship to Brenda, the home health care nurse?

The answer, of course, is that we are fascinated by high status. Since Aristotle, people of elevated status have served as the heroes in our dramas, because only someone who starts high up can fall from grace. In daily life, as in art, our eyes track the lives of the rich and famous and look right past the ordinary slouches to our left and right.

Why do we care so much about status? This is the point in most books where the argument is made that human beings are unique among the animal kingdom, but in this case the craving for status does not set us apart. In fact, it is such an ancient part of our nature that we share it with our primate cousins. Watching baboons or chimpanzees compete openly, physically, and sometimes violently for their position in the hierarchy feels simultaneously foreign and familiar to us. It's as uncomfortable as watching them mate: We feel embarrassed by their vulgarity and yet we recognize exactly what is driving them.

Nonhuman primates turn out to behave a lot like humans when it comes to celebrity gawking. In a study led by neuroscientist Michael Platt, rhesus macaque monkeys were given the option to look at different kinds of pictures while their eye movements were tracked. One set of photos included only high-ranking monkeys from their colony; a second set featured only low-ranking members. Each time the monkey looked at a picture, he got a squirt of fruit juice delivered through a straw. (To a thirsty macaque, a squirt of cold juice is a welcome treat that beats monkey chow any day.) The researchers systematically varied the amount of juice the monkeys received: Looking at the low-status photos would earn more juice than looking at the high-status ones.

The monkeys' preference was clear. They wanted to look at the high-status monkeys, and they would sacrifice a lot of juice to do so. In fact, they had to be paid extra juice to tolerate the sight of the low-status monkeys compared with looking at nothing but a blank screen. There was only one thing that the male monkeys wanted to see more than the celebrity monkeys, and that was the genitalia of female macaques.

What does the behavior of these monkeys have to do with us? To begin with, humans and macaques share about 93 percent of our DNA. That obviously does not mean that we are the same. But if you consider these observations of macaques together with a similar preoccupation with status across other primates like chimpanzees and baboons, which are even more closely related to us, you begin to see a continuous pattern. The last common ancestors of macaques and humans lived about twenty-five million years ago, much earlier than the six million to eight million years that separate us from our common ancestor with chimps. The similarity between humans and macaques in an obsession with status means that the trait was likely already present in our common ancestor, and as such is truly ancient.

Archaeologists tell us that for the vast majority of our evolutionary history, our ancestors lived in small groups who hunted for meat and gathered plants from the forests and savannas. This way of life lasted for at least a hundred thousand years, and during that time human societies were highly egalitarian, which we know from the fact that fossil remains and the artifacts found with them were all fairly similar from one person to another. When later societies became more hierarchical, kings and pharaohs would be found buried with mounds of treasures, and occasionally even their favorite dogs, wives, or slaves, while the graves of the lower classes might be found with nothing but a blanket, if they were lucky.

When I first learned about these egalitarian hunter-gatherers as a college student, I imagined them as a loving, peaceful, sharing people, almost like hippies in loincloths, uncorrupted by modern-day materialism. In reality, the main reason that hunter-gatherers were egalitarian was not that they were more benevolent than we are today, but rather that it was difficult to accumulate dramatically more wealth than others in a group given that there was no real wealth beyond today's kill or tomorrow's berry haul. Sharing simply made good sense. If I kill a mastodon, what am I going to do with all the meat? The best way to store it would be in the stomachs of my friends and family. There, it would become converted into the currency of goodwill, so that the next time I needed help, they would be there for me.

This system of reciprocal sharing works because people remembered. They remembered who got what and how much effort each person put in, and they got upset when some got more than others. A study of capuchin monkeys (the kind you've seen grinding music from an old-timey street organ) suggests that this talent for social accounting is also ancient. Like humans, monkeys become distraught when they get the wrong end of a deal. Primatologist Sarah Brosnan designed a simple exchange game with the capuchins. First, she would give a monkey a small stone. She would then hold out her hand, and when the monkey gave the stone back, she would give it a piece of cucumber. When they played this exchange game, the monkeys would consistently trade stones for cucumbers.

In the critical part of the experiment, Brosnan would include two monkeys in the game, so that they could watch each other's transactions. First, Brosnan would play with one monkey and exchange the stone for a cucumber slice. Then she would play the same game with the second monkey, but instead reward the exchange with a grape—considered by the monkeys to be a much better snack than a cucumber. Brosnan now went back to the first monkey and tried the original game again to determine whether it would make the "rational" choice (in a narrow economic sense) and take the cucumber, since some food is better than no food. Or would it do the more socially intelligent thing and protest, giving up nutrients in order to enforce a code of fairness?

This time the shortchanged monkey was having none of it: It looked at the cucumber slice, then threw it back at Brosnan. This sequence was played out dozens of times with many different pairs of monkeys. Sometimes the subject would simply toss the cucumber away, and at other times it would fling it back in the experimenter's face. Sometimes the monkey would not even return the stone. Why pay for inferior quality?

The cucumber, which had been acceptable a few minutes earlier, was no longer good enough when the next guy over was getting grapes. These results were remarkable, because they showed that monkeys cared more about where they stood compared with other monkeys than about their actual, tangible, edible rewards. Their sense of fairness was more sophisticated than many had assumed.

Primatologists are careful not to describe in human terms the internal states of the animals they study. So when a monkey jumps up and down, bares its teeth, and lunges aggressively, primatologists might call it an "aggression display," but they would not say that the monkey was angry. If you watch the video of Brosnan's experiment being conducted, though, it is hard not to interpret the monkeys' behavior as expressing an emotion. They throw the cucumber back at the experimenter, then shake the front of their cages and call out like a prisoner starting a riot. I'm not a primatologist, so I can say it: Those monkeys are mad.

The discovery that capuchin monkeys are averse to receiving unequal outcomes, much like humans, suggests that these tendencies are evolved rather than learned. If people really are born caring about equality, then we should be able to find evidence of it even in young children. And, in fact, children as young as three years old do show reactions much like those of the capuchins. For example, one study asked pairs of children to help an experimenter clean up some blocks. As a reward, the experimenter gave them some stickers. Sometimes the rewards were equal, and sometimes one child received more stickers than the other. Even though they could not yet verbalize that the unequal share was unfair, the children became visibly upset when they received less than their partner. As every parent of preschoolers knows, they do not need to be taught that receiving the same amount is fair but receiving less is unfair. It may take time to learn to count, but they seem to have an innate notion of fairness.

Early human groups almost certainly had a status hierarchy, with some people ranking higher than others. But without the ability to accrue significant amounts of wealth, and with populations numbering in the dozens rather than the thousands, it was simply impossible for the difference between the top and the bottom of the hierarchy to be very big. Like our primate relatives, early humans would have cared deeply about status within their small bands. The natural social structure of early *Homo sapiens* was a Status Ladder, but it was a very short one.

What changed since then was not human nature. What changed instead was very practical, very concrete, and very recent: Humans invented farming. After a thousand centuries during which hunting and gathering was the only way of life, agriculture appeared a mere hundred centuries ago at more or less the same time in many places around the planet. On an evolutionary time scale, this is a blink of an eye. Suddenly, for the first time, people were able to settle in one place, plant crops, and store the harvest, such as in the form of clay pots full of grain. Humans also began to raise livestock, which, from the herder's point of view, are walking meat storage devices. Once food could be accumulated in large quantities, it became possible for some people to amass a lot more of it than others. And they did. It was not long before cities sprang up in places like Egypt, the Middle East, China, India, and the Americas. Along with these larger, denser, agricultural societies, wealth inequality began to climb.

While it is hard to determine the extent of economic inequality in ancient times, we can guess that it was extremely high. Most large ancient agricultural societies had a king or other ruler with the power to command vast fortunes. On the low end of the social scale, the majority of ordinary people were peasants, and slavery was commonly practiced. In modern history, income inequality reached its highest point in the late 1920s, immediately before the stock market crash of 1929 and the Great Depression that followed—its highest point, that is, until today. We have now reached the same level of inequality that existed prior to the Great Depression.

If humans are not unique when it comes to caring about status, one distinction that we can claim is that we have built social ladders of such height that they dwarf those of our primate relatives and ancient hunter-gatherers. This quantitative difference sets the stage for conflicts between the scale of inequality in which we evolved and the scale that we confront today.

So much depends on how we understand the disparities between the haves and the have-nots. If you ask people whether they believe there is too much inequality or not, their answers will be biased by their own positions. People who are struggling will tend to say the level of inequality is excessive, but those who have benefited from the current system will state that it seems to be working just fine. How can we establish how much inequality is "too much"?

The most important insight into that question took shape in an elegant home in Baltimore in 1928. John, the seven-year-old son of William Lee Rawls, had contracted diphtheria, a respiratory infection with symptoms similar to those of the flu. Unlike the flu, however, diphtheria kills up to 20 percent of children who contract it. But William Rawls's son had the best medical care money could buy, as his father was one of the most prominent attorneys in Baltimore. With constant care, John recovered—but not before he'd passed the infection to his younger brother, Bobby. Bobby was less fortunate; he died before his sixth birthday.

A year later young John was bedridden again, this time with pneumonia. Again he recovered. But now he passed the infection to his two-year-old brother, Tommy. Again, the younger boy died.

John Rawls grew up to become the most important political philosopher of the twentieth century. His biographer argues that the heartbreaking deaths of his brothers were the most influential events of Rawls's life. Maybe his younger siblings were less hardy than John; maybe they were simply less lucky. Rawls himself was endowed not only with a strong immune system, but also with a brilliant intellect and unwavering discipline. Most of us think of these as admirable qualities that should earn anyone who possesses them a well-deserved place in the upper echelons of a meritocratic society.

John Rawls, however, was deeply suspicious of that idea. If a man is brilliant, he argued, why should he be praised for being so? He was merely fortunate for being born intelligent. If he has a strong work ethic, he just happened to win the lottery for hardworking traits. And if one boy was strong enough to survive a terrible disease and a weaker boy succumbed, that was merely a brutal fact of life. Rawls saw nothing just or morally praiseworthy in that.

The most famous part of Rawls's theory of justice was a thought experiment called "the veil of ignorance." Imagine that you have awakened from a deep sleep on an interstellar space flight, and you remember nothing about yourself. You don't know if you are rich or poor. You don't know if you are strong or weak, smart or dim-witted. As your spacecraft nears a new planet, you have to choose in which of many societies you would like to live. The problem is, you have no idea what kind of position you will occupy in the group you select.

Some of these alien societies are incredibly unequal, with slavery being the norm. Others are not quite as imbalanced, but their inequality is still extreme, with some of the inhabitants desperately poor while others are fabulously rich. Still other societies are egalitarian, with only small differences between the haves and the have-nots. Which would you pick?

Some daring souls might choose an unequal society and gamble on landing in a privileged position. But Rawls argued that any reasonable person would choose an egalitarian society, which would ensure that even the worst possible outcome would be tolerable. Rawls's insight was that if you simply ask people how much inequality they judge to be just or unjust, their opinions will be biased by their abilities and self-interest. The strongest, smartest, most competitive individuals will advocate for more unequal outcomes because they are starting with an advantage. Likewise, those with the worst prospects would opt for a more equal distribution. So, instead of expressing what they believe to be fair and just, people would opt for what benefits them. Although no one can eliminate the biasing influences of his own position entirely, Rawls thought that the exercise of peering through the veil of ignorance would enable us to see more objectively than we otherwise could.

The veil of ignorance is only a thought experiment, of course, but a study by psychologist Michael Norton and behavioral economist

Dan Ariely went a step further to apply it to actual data. They divided the population into five equal quintiles, from the poorest 20 percent to the richest 20 percent, and then asked a subject group of more than five thousand Americans to estimate what portion of the country's total wealth was owned by each segment. While people in the study recognized that there was inequality, their responses indicated that they greatly underestimated its extremity. For example, they judged that the wealthiest fifth had about 59 percent of the nation's wealth, when in reality it has 84 percent.

Then, using the same five quintiles, the researchers asked participants to describe what they thought the allotments *should* be in an ideal world. The test subjects allocated the wealthiest quintile in this scenario about a third of the wealth, and the poorest group about 10 percent. (In reality, the true share for the bottom quintile is 0.1 percent.) These ideal allotments did not look much like those of the United States, the most unequal developed nation in the world. Instead, they resembled those of Sweden, one of the most equal nations on earth.

The most interesting part of the study was what the researchers did next. They showed the subjects a pair of pie charts illustrating two different wealth distributions. Although the participants did not know it, one represented the actual distribution in the United States, and the other that of Sweden. They asked them to pick which society they would rather live in, if they were going to be randomly assigned to end up in any economic status in that society. In other words, they placed participants behind Rawls's veil of ignorance and let them choose.

A striking 92 percent of Americans chose the Swedish model. Even more surprising was the amount of consensus in that choice. Both men and women selected Sweden by more than a 90 percent margin. People who made six-figure salaries selected Sweden almost as often (89 percent) as those who made less than $50,000

(92 percent). There was even consensus across political lines, as the Swedish chart was chosen overwhelmingly by both Republicans (90 percent) and Democrats (94 percent). Forty years after Rawls proposed the concept of the veil of ignorance, people behaved just as he predicted any reasonable person would.

Rawls used the veil of ignorance to argue that once self-interest is removed, anyone can see that equality *ought to be* preferable to inequality. Norton and Ariely's study confirmed that most people do in fact favor equality—up to a point. Subjects did not choose complete equality: They still believed the top fifth should have a far greater proportion of the total wealth than the bottom fifth. But the difference between our current reality and what people judge it ought to be means that we find ourselves in a curious predicament. Our modern economy proves to be an uncomfortable fit for the kinds of creatures we have become over the last thousand centuries or so.

Mismatches between slowly evolving appetites on the one hand and quickly changing environments on the other are a source of much misery in the modern world. Take hunger, for instance. Evolution does not rely on an organism to reason its way from "I need a certain number of calories to survive" to "therefore I shall eat this particular food." Thinking is too complicated, too unreliable, and not urgent enough for that. Instead, nature just builds in a taste for that kind of food. We evolved a craving for nutrients such as sugar and fat because they are highly effective for packing on weight. Food was scarce enough for our hunter-gatherer ancestors that the threat of starving greatly outweighed any potential downsides of eating too much. An early human with a ravenous appetite for sugar and fat would tend to outcompete others with less voracious appetites. As a result, that trait spread through the population. But in today's world, where food is plentiful, such cravings contribute to obesity, diabetes, and heart disease. Nature even built in a helpful delay between the time our stomach is full and the time our brain gets the satiation signal, which helped ensure that our ancestors would eat a little extra at each meal. The trouble is, that mechanism still works.

The same kinds of mismatches wreak havoc in our sex lives. Evolution did not rely on individuals to make family planning decisions in order to pass on their genes. Instead, it simply fashioned some kinds of humans to be irresistible to other kinds of humans. And then it built us in such a way that the activities that happen to feel eye-rollingly, toe-quiveringly ecstatic are also the activities that tend to create babies. In one respect, that system seems to have been a huge success, as the global population has recently swelled past seven billion. But consider that half of all pregnancies, and 80 percent of teenage pregnancies, in the United States are unintended. Or contemplate the fact that about 25 percent of married people admit to having had an extramarital affair. We have to question the suitability of the fit between our stone-age sexuality and contemporary realities. Our gene-reproducing system may be too successful for how we would like to live today, and we might be able to avoid a lot of grief if certain other people were just a little more resistible.

There is likewise a mismatch between our evolved yearning for status and our modern economic environment. As we will see in the next chapter, high status comes with many benefits for both survival and reproduction. Our ancestors who were status strivers left behind more descendants than their more languid competitors. As a result, they bequeathed to us a visceral appetite for status. Money, power, and the admiration of other people seem just as irresistible to many people as food and sex. The meek may eventually inherit the earth, but the proud have been in firm possession of it so far.

For thousands of centuries the social ladders our minds and bodies have evolved to climb were only a few rungs high. If the contemporary world's ladder were still on the kind of human scale to which we were once accustomed, then our urge for status might not be a problem, but instead we are facing the equivalent of scaling skyscrapers. Likewise, if we were a species that didn't care much about status, then today's massive inequality might be tolerable. But our intrinsic appetite for high status crashes against the towering inequality we see around us with enormous consequences for everyone, not just the poor, but the middle class as well.

The free lunches, food stamps, and government cheese that marked my childhood were objective signals indicating my family's rung on the Status Ladder. But the disorientation I felt standing in the fourth-grade lunch line was not based on a calculation about money. It was my subjective perception snapping into line with the reality of a new Status Ladder.

When we examine the human hunger for social status, together with the fact that many of the world's economies have become extraordinarily unequal in recent decades, our perspective on inequality changes. If our response to inequality is shaped by our need for status, then inequality is not simply a matter of how much money we have; it's about where we stand compared with other people. Money, from that perspective, is simply one way we keep score. *Feeling* poor matters, not just *being* poor. That is why your subjective standing on the Status Ladder reveals so much about what you are likely to become.

Chapter 2

Relatively Easy

Why We Can't Stop Comparing Ourselves to Others

Mollie Orshansky never intended to draw the official line that separated the have-nots from the haves. She grew up on the wrong side of that line herself, one of six sisters sleeping two to a bed in the Bronx. She was the first in her family of Ukrainian immigrants to complete high school, and then college. She never dreamed that a series of numbers that she calculated by hand and arranged in neat columns in the pages of an obscure journal would come to define for millions of people the curious concept of *enough*.

In the 1960s Orshansky worked as a staff researcher for the Social Security Administration, looking for better ways to quantify poverty from census data. Before her work, it was difficult to establish how many poor people there were in the United States, because few metrics existed to count them. One of Orshansky's ideas was to classify families as poor based on the cost of food. She knew that the average family at the time spent a third of its income on food. It happened that the Department of Agriculture had recently released four family food plans, each one describing a set of staple supplies that a family would need for healthy meals. The plans were ordered from the most expensive (the "liberal" plan) to the least expensive one that a family could survive on (the "thrifty" plan). So, in a 1963 paper, Orshansky proposed that researchers might define poverty by taking the second least expensive meal plan and multiplying its cost by three. Enough, in that formulation, would be defined as being just able to feed your family and cover basic expenses. Incomes that fell below that number would be considered below the poverty line.

In 1964 Lyndon Johnson declared the "War on Poverty." Because the administration lacked an official metric to define who was poor, it decided to adopt a version of the "Orshansky index" to determine who was eligible for government benefits and who was not. Mollie Orshansky was as surprised as anybody about this decision. She had developed her method to help researchers measure poverty and never meant for it to be used to determine who received benefits. Although she favored using the second cheapest meal plan as the basis for the index, the government wanted to use the least expensive. In response, she tried to add a little padding into the budget by suggesting that an additional fifteen cents per day be included for occasional treats for children, or a cup of coffee. In her tinkering you can see the traces of someone who had lived with poverty. "When I write about poverty," she once said, "I don't have to have a good imagination. I have a good memory." Her supervisor ultimately vetoed her suggestion and the government opted for the least expensive meal plan, officially setting the poverty line as three times the food expenses of the cheapest possible way to feed a family.

That same formula is still the way the U.S. government defines poverty today. The index is adjusted for inflation, but not for changes in the kinds of expenses families have. Those changes have had a major impact over the years. For example, in the 1960s families spent a third of their income on food and paid for everything else with the remaining two thirds. Today, however, average Americans spend only about 13 percent of their incomes on food. Other costs have skyrocketed, so that the other 87 percent covers needs like housing, transportation, child care, and health care. To make the poverty line have an equivalent meaning now as it did when it was invented, you would have to multiply the minimum food cost by eight, not three.

Today the poverty line is $23,850 a year for a family of four, whether that family lives in New York City or on a country road in Arkansas. And yet, when a 2013 Gallup poll asked Americans what they thought was the smallest income that would allow a family of four to get by, the average answer was $58,000. Their answers were relative to the respondents' own incomes. Households earning less than $30,000 said it took about $44,000 to get by, but those earning $75,000 or more said it took at least $69,000 to do so. When Gallup asked how much it took to be rich, the median answer was $150,000. But this answer again depended on the respondents' own income. The more a person made, the more he believed it took to be considered rich. For most people, being rich seems to mean making about three times as much as they actually earn.

So who *is* really poor, and who is not? The answer to that question is more complicated than it seems. Consider recent government surveys reporting that, among American households below the federal poverty line, 96 percent have televisions, 93 percent have microwaves, 83 percent have air-conditioning, and 81 percent have a cell phone. Can a cell phone–using, microwave-cooking channel flipper really be described as being poor?

Let's look at the question from another angle. Thomas Jefferson, the third president of the United States and the author of the Declaration of Independence, lived in luxury. He built Monticello, one of the most celebrated homes of his day. Monticello was innovative not only for its architecture, but also for its clever gadgets, which were ahead of their time, many of which were invented by Jefferson himself. Take, for example, the "polygraph" in Jefferson's home office. It was not a lie detector, as we use the term today, but rather a mechanical contraption with a writing pad and a series of wooden levers connecting two fountain pens. When you wrote a letter with one pen, it simultaneously made a copy with the other. Then there were the dumbwaiters, tiny elevators operated by a set of pulleys to deliver dinners between floors, and Jefferson's "Great Clock," whose intricate gears could not only tell the time, but also the day and the month.

Despite these technical marvels, Jefferson had no hot water, no air-conditioning, no electricity, and certainly no microwaves. By material standards, he would be judged to be poorer than the poor in today's developed countries. Why, then, do we not regard him as having been poor? Because, as the historical perspective makes clear, poverty and wealth are always relative to what other people have in a particular time and place.

Adam Smith made this very point in *The Wealth of Nations*:

> By necessaries I understand, not only the commodities which are indispensably necessary for the support of life, but whatever the custom of the country renders it indecent for creditable people, even of the lowest order, to be without. A linen shirt, for example, is, strictly speaking, not a necessary of life. . . . But in the present times, through the greater part of Europe, a creditable day-labourer would be ashamed to appear in public without a linen shirt . . . Custom, in the same manner, has rendered leather shoes a necessary of life in England. The poorest creditable person of either sex would be ashamed to appear in public without them.

Yesterday's linen shirt is today's smartphone. More than two hundred years ago, the father of economics reasoned his way to a conclusion that modern science is proving today. Poverty and wealth are not just about absolute sums of money. In countries developed enough that the poor are not actually starving, the key factor is relative position. To understand why this is the case, we have to examine how the human mind judges value in the most fundamental ways.

Take a look at the checkerboard tiles in Figure 2.1 below. It would be impossible for me to convince you that the gray square labeled A is identical in brightness to the square labeled B. And yet, it is. Spend a few minutes reasoning with your eyeballs, squinting and slanting any way you wish, and you will not be able to make the illusion go away. Your brain is doing exactly what a good visual system ought to do, which is to take context into account. Because your brain knows that objects look darker when they are in shadow than in the light, it compensates for the shadow cast by the cylinder by saying, "If B looks this bright in shadow, it must be much brighter in reality."

The reason psychologists are fascinated by visual illusions is that they enable us to catch an occasional glimpse of the clever tricks our minds use by experiencing the clash between what we know to be true and how things seem to us. In the case of the checkerboard illusion, our perception is biased, and we make an error. But the bias exists for a good reason: In real life, objects really *do* look darker in shadow, so a visual system built to account for that fact will end up perceiving things more accurately in the wild.

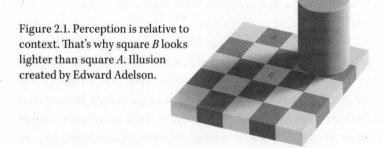

Figure 2.1. Perception is relative to context. That's why square *B* looks lighter than square *A*. Illusion created by Edward Adelson.

This dependence on context is not unique to vision, but is central to the way our brains perceive just about anything. Consider the sensation of hunger. Knowing when to eat and when we feel full is such a fundamental biological necessity that we surely must have evolved an exquisitely sensitive internal calorimeter, right? Wrong. Our feelings of hunger and satiation are shaped to an astonishing extent by context.

Take a plate and pile it high with ribs, as they do at The Pig, my favorite barbecue joint. Then, halfway through finishing this meal, ask a diner to rate how full he is, and he will tend to give you a rating near the middle of the scale. Now, take two little ribs and place them in the middle of a plate—maybe stack them vertically and add some microgreens—the way they might be served at a high-end restaurant. Then try the same exercise and ask the diner in the middle of his meal how full he feels. He will tend to give you the same midway rating as those in the barbecue joint, even though he's actually eaten much less.

People judge how full they are not simply on the calories they have consumed, but on what proportion of the whole they have eaten. The most elegant demonstration of this was a study led by Brian Wansink at Cornell University. His team rigged some soup bowls with a tube attached to their bottoms, which ran through the tabletop and to a big cauldron of tomato soup. As diners ate, more soup could imperceptibly flow into the bowls through the tube, keeping it at a constant level. The Olive Garden claims to have a never-ending pasta bowl, but the Wansink lab invented the first truly bottomless bowl of soup.

The researchers then invited groups of research participants to a free lunch. The subjects were seated at tables for four. Although they didn't know it, two of the bowls were regular bowls, and the other two were bottomless. They were asked to eat as much as they liked, and then to estimate how much they had eaten and how full they were. Although those with bottomless bowls ate nearly twice as much as those with regular bowls, they believed that they had eaten the same amount. Even more surprisingly, the two groups felt equally full. Their sensation of being sated was shaped more by their perception of how much they had eaten than by the actual calories consumed. Their perception of how much they had eaten was driven by how full their bowl appeared to be with respect to the size of the bowl.

The other night I opened my refrigerator and reached for the milk. For some reason, I slammed the half-empty gallon container against the roof of the fridge so hard that it hurt my hand and brought my daughter running in from the next room. I was as surprised as she was by my action and tried to explain, "Um, need more milk." Although I had no conscious thoughts about the weight of milk in the carton before I lifted it, I must have expected a full gallon, because that's what my arm muscles were prepared to lift.

Many studies have shown that expectations and context shape perceptions of weight. A gallon of milk feels lighter if you've just lifted a bag full of groceries than if you've just lifted a marshmallow. This relativity in judgments of weight had been demonstrated so often that by the 1950s it was regarded as a fundamental law that governed how the brain transformed raw sensory data (like muscle tension) into subjective perceptions of heft. And then one study made everyone rethink their assumptions.

Donald Brown was a graduate student at Berkeley in the early 1950s when he conducted an experiment that appeared, for the most part, to resemble the hundreds of previous studies showing that perceptual judgments were relative. After lining up a series of little brass weights, he asked research participants to pick them up and describe them on a scale from "very light" to "very heavy." Following the procedure of many previous studies, Brown varied the sequence of the weights. When the participants picked up a heavy weight and then a lighter one, the latter felt especially light by comparison. When they picked up a light weight and then a heavy one, the second one felt especially heavy.

Then, halfway through the study, Brown slyly asked the participants to pick up a tray full of weights and set it aside so that they could go on to judging the next set of weights. The loaded tray was itself, of course, a heavy weight. But when they picked up the next weight, lifting the tray did not affect their judgment of its heft. How can it be that lifting a single heavy weight affects weight perception, but lifting a group of heavy weights does not?

That paradox couldn't happen if the relativity effect was an immutable physiological law governing the translation of muscle tension into perceptions of weight. This was an early clue that the comparisons we make are more sophisticated than we commonly assume. We not only make constant comparisons, but we make subtle assumptions about which comparisons count and which ones don't.

We are so accustomed to judging social status that it comes automatically to us, like riding a bicycle or driving after years of practice. As I write this, I'm sitting in a crowded coffee shop on a cool winter morning. At the tables around me are a cross section of the population of this college town. There's a fifty-year-old man with silver hair and tortoiseshell glasses, a sweater zipped up over his pressed button-down shirt. He's with his three teenage children, who somehow exude confidence even though they are in T-shirts and baseball caps. Then there is the pair of twenty-somethings. He wears thick black-rimmed glasses and a black pullover, the bright North Face logo the most visible part of his clothing. He is constantly checking his smartphone. She is beautiful, in fitted jeans and sweater, with sunglasses pushed atop her perfectly groomed hair and earrings that match her bracelet. Next to them, a slightly older pair of twentysomethings are leaning close, talking intensely. She has messy blond hair falling over the colorful patterned scarf around her neck, which is layered over a sweater with another pattern. He wears a blue flannel shirt and has a fuzzy beard and fuzzy hair. They seem to have rolled out of bed together not long ago.

If you walk into any coffee shop like this one, it seems a fairly straightforward task to guess people's social class. It seems like a skill that would take years to master. But perhaps not. One day when my daughter was three, she pointed to a girl in her day care class photo, which hung on the wall in our house. "Ellie is rich like me," she announced, matter-of-factly. Stunned by this statement, I asked, pointing to another child, "What about this one?" "Oh," my daughter said, "she's poor."

Now I was intrigued. My daughter attends a day care run by the university where I teach. Everyone who attends the program is affiliated with the university in some way. After three years of drop-offs, pickups, playdates, and birthday parties, I knew the families in her class well enough to know all the parents' occupations. Many of them are professors or physicians; others are graduate students or staff members.

I directed my daughter's attention back to the class photo, and for every one of the fifteen children, she labeled them "rich" if their parents were professors or physicians, and "poor" if their parents were students or staff members. Objectively speaking, none of the families would be classified as "poor" according to a metric like the Orshansky index. But my daughter was judging relative to herself and her professor parents, and by that criterion, she had perfect accuracy. Was she just lucky? Not likely. The probability of making the right guess fifteen times in a row by chance is about three in one hundred thousand. I felt a strange blend of pride and mortification. Was my daughter especially astute? Or was she unusually obsessed with status? In reality, she was probably neither. Studies show that identifying other people's social class really is child's play for most of us.

Psychologists Michael Kraus and Dacher Keltner tested how accurately adults can judge social class by asking fifty-three pairs of college students who did not know one another to chat for five minutes while their conversation was video-recorded. (Let's call these participants the Chatters.) They then showed a one-minute clip from each video to a second set of research participants, who were asked to guess the social class of each person in the video by rating them on the Status Ladder that we saw in Chapter 1. (We'll call them the Raters.)

After viewing just a short sample of behavior, the Raters' impressions of the Chatters were remarkably accurate: Their placement of the Chatters on the Status Ladder correlated significantly with the Chatters' own self-reported family income and their parents' education level. The researchers coded the videotapes to see what characteristics of the Chatters might be communicating their class differences. They found that richer Chatters were more disengaged during the conversation. They spent more time grooming themselves, doodling, and fiddling with pens, phones, or other objects. The poorer Chatters, in contrast, were more engaged. They looked directly at their conversation partner, and they nodded and laughed more. Higher status meant that the richer participants didn't have anything "on the line" in the conversation. The poorer participants, in contrast, were working harder to be liked and accepted.

Research like Kraus's study shows that social status can be perceived quickly and intuitively with very little information. But another kind of study has indicated that people can actually make social comparisons between themselves and others without any awareness of doing so. One of the most reliable findings in social psychology is that if you consciously think about a person who is clearly superior to you in some respect, it makes you feel worse about yourself than if you had never given that person any thought. Likewise, if you think about someone who is inferior to you in some way, it makes you feel better about yourself by comparison. A team of psychologists led by Thomas Mussweiler asked whether this same social comparison effect could occur unconsciously.

The researchers asked study participants to rate their own athletic abilities using questions like: "How many push-ups can you do?" or "How long would it take you to run a one-hundred-meter dash?" But before they answered those questions, the participants were asked to reflect on their athletic prowess for one minute while staring at a computer monitor that contained a string of random letters. What participants didn't know was that ten times during that minute, the letter string was actually replaced with the name of a famous person for fifteen thousandths of a second. At that duration, the name couldn't be consciously perceived, so any effect it had was subliminal.

One group of participants was exposed to the name "Michael Jordan," while the second group was exposed to "Pope John Paul." Mussweiler assumed that people would consider the pontiff less athletic than the basketball star, and, as expected, the participants rated their own athletic abilities better after being subliminally exposed to the pope than to Jordan. Whatever comparison process was driving this effect must have happened unconsciously, because the participants were not aware that they had even read the names against which they were comparing themselves.

Think what these studies mean for our daily experience. One minute, you're sitting at a sidewalk café, enjoying a cup of coffee and thumbing through a magazine, feeling pretty satisfied with yourself. And then you start to wonder: *Am I as successful as I ought to be at my age? I'll bet Cheryl in the office makes more than I do. Should I put hardwoods in my kitchen?* Although the thoughts seem to come to mind out of nowhere, they are usually the outcome of a process going on behind the scenes of consciousness.

Just as in the Michael Jordan example above, you may have been primed by the Tiffany ad you didn't even notice as you flipped the page, or by the Porsche that drove by while you were stirring in the sugar.

You don't question the whiteness of the magazine page in front of you or the blackness of the ink, even though perceptions of light and dark can be shaped by context, as in the checkerboard illusion. You don't question the weight of the paper the magazine is printed on, even though it would feel different had you just lifted your chair rather than your coffee cup. You don't question the sensation in your gut that tells you that you want another coffee, even though that desire might be shaped by the size of your mug. *This is black. That is white. I'd like another cup of coffee, and an upgraded kitchen.* We are aware of these thoughts and emotions that are the culmination of the brain's computations, yet we remain unaware of those unconscious computations themselves, as the brain constantly monitors the context, makes comparisons, and simply announces its outcomes. As a result, we can end up feeling inferior or superior without any awareness we were doing any comparing at all.

One clue that you have been unconsciously comparing yourself to others is that you find yourself being competitive about something that's not even important to you. On Wednesdays in a little conference room in Chapel Hill, you can find seven professors, two decks of cards, and a painted wooden pumpkin filled with good chocolate. My colleagues and I eat lunch together there while playing Oh Hell and chatting about the issues of the day. Sometimes it's dry department business; sometimes it's juicy gossip. And then there are the days when the room is silent, our eyes flickering between cards because the game is close.

There's no money on the line. In fact, victory is slightly ignoble, because when the game is over, the winner has to carry the painted pumpkin down the hall to its home, enduring students' bemused looks. Yet the game is always intense: there is something impossible to resist about the possibility of proving oneself better than someone else, if only for an hour, if only in the silliest of ways.

Why do my colleagues and I engage in such intense competition even when there is no financial gain involved? Because, from the brain's perspective, there is not much difference between money and relative status. Both are processed using the same areas of the brain, which are sometimes called the "reward circuit." The reward circuit is a set of interconnected brain regions whose neurons fire when we get something we want, or are about to. The "reward" language comes from research with rats and mice. Put a hungry rat in a cage and give it a food pellet every time it paws a button, and before long the rat is pressing the button as if it were a slot machine.

If this particular rat happens to have a wire implanted through his skull into a particular place in the middle of the brain, it will register electrical impulses from his neurons during this process. If you hook up that wire to a speaker, then you can hear the neurons going *snap, crackle, pop* like radio static. At first, the sound will be low and sporadic, but as he reaches for the button and the treat begins to appear, the noise will crescendo. Once the pellet is eaten, it fades away again. The more intense the crackling for a given treat, the more keenly he will work the button for another one.

The strong link between electrical activity in the reward circuit and the intense "More, please!" response gave James Olds and Peter Milner, neuroscientists at McGill University, an ingenious idea. From the food reward experiments, there seemed to be a closed loop: Press the button, a snack appears, the reward center starts firing, and the animal starts pressing for more. One way to interpret this loop is to say that the brain's electrical activity is a means of assuring that past successful button pressing will be repeated. Another way to look at it, though, is to say that the button pressing and food eating is just a means by which the brain can stimulate itself. In other words, maybe brain stimulation in this area is rewarding in itself, and eating is just a way to trigger it.

Olds and Milner asked what would happen if the food treat was removed altogether, and instead the button was hooked up to a battery that would stimulate the brain directly. When they did this, the rats pressed the lever compulsively. In later versions of the experiment, they would not only forgo both food and water to keep pressing the button, but would cross an electrified floor, enduring painful shocks to their feet, to get to the button. The electrical stimulation was so efficient at providing their brains with reward signals that the rats had no need for anything else. They would keep hitting that button until they collapsed from exhaustion.

If you are thinking that this brain stimulation apparatus would be delightful and that you'd like to try it sometime, I've got a suggestion: Spare yourself the brain surgery and have a beer instead. The brain pathways of the reward circuit evolved to make us keep seeking out things that are good for survival and reproduction—that is to say, things like food and sex. But substances that give people a high, from an earthy Pinot to crack cocaine, all stimulate this same brain network, as they happen to have chemical structures that mimic the brain's natural reward-signaling chemicals. When you have a few drinks, you are achieving the same result chemically that Olds and Milner's rats were attaining electrically.

To study humans, of course, we don't listen to the noises from wires implanted in the brain. Instead, we look at the colorful brain maps produced from functional MRI scans. If you watch these brain scans while people eat chocolate, enjoy a martini, or (rather awkwardly) have sex, you will see the same reward circuitry buzzing to life. Because the same brain network responds to all these very different kinds of experiences, the reward net-work creates a kind of "common currency" across many different kinds of stimuli. You may not be surprised, then, to learn that it responds the same way when we make money. Dozens of studies have shown that when research participants gamble, pick stocks, or make financial decisions and earn money doing so, the reward circuit responds just as it does for food, sex, or drugs.

The strange finding, though, is that it responds just as strongly to relative status as it does to actual money. Consider an experiment led by neuroscientist Klaus Fliessbach. Volunteers in the study had their brains scanned while they played a simple game in pairs. In each round of the game players made decisions, such as identifying which of two pictures had more dots on it. There was not enough time to actually count, so they had to make a quick estimate. When they got it right, players won money, and after each decision the computer showed how much each player earned.

There was every reason to expect that the reward circuit would be abuzz when players won money. But the real question in this study was whether the reward circuit "cared" about rela-tive status, and indeed that proved to be the case. Regardless of the actual amount of money the player won, the reward circuit was activated more strongly when the player won more than the other player. Simply knowing they were doing better than other players drew the same brain responses as sex, money, or drugs. Status is clearly a powerful motivator, and studies like this sug-gest that when we say people crave status, "craving" is more than a metaphor.

As we've seen, people effortlessly judge everything from light-ness to heaviness to social class by relative comparison; they assess other people's status at a glance; and they physically crave to be higher than others on the Status Ladder. Put these together, and you have a recipe for a species that is incredibly sensitive not simply to material wealth, but to inequality itself. We've also seen that, when it comes to something as basic as food, the stomach and brain can't accurately judge when we have had enough. More abstract judgments, like whether we have sufficient money, a big enough house, or a nice enough car, must be shaped even more by relative comparisons, as we have no sensors for this hunger, no taste buds for these tastes. How, then, do we judge "enough" in everyday life where status is concerned?

In a now famous study to determine how much money is enough, economists Andrew Clark and Andrew Oswald analyzed data from more than five thousand British households. A survey had asked them a series of questions about how satisfied they were with their jobs in general and their pay in particular. The data also included detailed information about each participant's occupation, salary, years of experience, and number of hours worked per week.

Classic economics textbooks treat work as a commodity that can be bought and sold for a particular price according to the laws of supply and demand. From this perspective, standard economic theory makes some seemingly obvious predictions. It says that people will be more satisfied when they make more money, and when they work fewer hours for it. But strangely, when Clark and Oswald looked at the relationship between income and satisfaction, the people in the top fifth of earners were slightly less satisfied than those in the bottom fifth, and the number of hours worked made little difference in their satisfaction. This made no sense.

Why might people be less satisfied when they are paid more? One reason is that, as you climb the ladder, your comparisons change. "Beggars do not envy millionaires," said Bertrand Russell, "though of course they will envy other beggars who are more successful." If you are in the top fifth of earners, the sky is the limit on who you might consider comparable. If you are a family doctor who makes $200,000 a year, you might feel unsatisfied when you measure yourself against a brain surgeon who makes $1 million a year. This, of course, assumes that relative comparison trumps cold hard cash in its power to satisfy.

To test that assumption, the economists looked at how each person's income compared to others in a similar job. They made use of a massive database of average pay rates for people in various occupational categories. If, for example, they were considering a forty-five-year-old lab technician with a college degree, in order to calculate relative income they would look up what the average lab technician of that age and that educational level made. They found that relative income had a substantial effect on satisfaction levels. The workers' actual pay barely mattered, nor did the number of hours worked. Those who were paid better than their peers were the most satisfied.

The importance of relative income has since been demonstrated in many studies around the world. Using economic data to measure satisfaction is one of the most direct ways to assess the effects of social comparisons on what people consider to be "enough." But the effects of relative differences have repercussions beyond just the subjective feelings of satisfaction. Poverty and wealth affect just about every aspect of daily life. We all know the many problems associated with poverty, which is why, when we have the choice, we prefer to live in nicer neighborhoods and to put our children in affluent school districts.

If relative comparisons are as important as I've argued, then some curious consequences should follow. If the brain depends on relative comparisons for even the most basic perceptions, then it must also do so with respect to affluence. And if our brains and bodies are attuned to relative comparisons, then the degree of inequality around us—not just our actual wealth—must play a key role in every area of life where wealth and poverty matter. As we shall see, it does.

Epidemiologists Richard Wilkinson and Kate Pickett surveyed the vast medical literature on the relationship between
wealth and a variety of social ills. They included homicides and
violent crime, school achievement and dropout rates, teenage
births, life expectancy and infant mortality, obesity, mental illness, and more—exactly the kinds of issues that are worse among
the poor. They compared the rates of these problems across all
the wealthy nations where the data were available. What they
found was astonishing.

If you consider all of the world's countries, the average income
per person is strongly linked to life expectancy and susceptibility
to social problems like crime. Desperately poor countries, like
Mozambique, fare much worse than wealthy countries, like England.
But when you examine only economically developed countries, like
the nations of Western Europe, the United States, Canada, and
Japan, the link breaks: Once people are wealthy enough that their
basic needs are met, additional income does not protect them from
bad life outcomes.

Consider homicide rates. Because we are used to thinking about
these social issues as problems of the poor, it seems obvious that violent crimes should be high in less affluent countries, like Portugal,
Spain, and Greece, whose annual incomes averaged around $20,000
per person, and lower in rich countries, like the United States, Norway, and Canada, where income averages are much higher. In fact,
there was no significant link between average income and homicide
rates. The same was true of life expectancy, infant mortality, obesity, and mental illness. In fact, of the ten social and health problems that Wilkinson and Pickett analyzed, only two—educational
achievement and trust in neighbors—showed any correlation with
income. When the ten measures were averaged together into a general index of health and social problems, there was no correlation to
income, as you can see in Figure 2.2. The countries form a vague
cloud with no clear pattern.

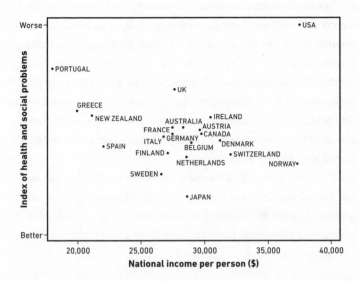

Figure 2.2. Index of health and social problems is not strongly associated with average income in developed nations. Adapted from Wilkinson and Pickett (2009).

One striking thing about this graph is that three countries rank high above the others—the United States, the United Kingdom, and Portugal—even though they are high, middle, and low on average income. On the bottom you can see a mirror image, with Sweden, Japan, and Norway strikingly low on social problems despite their wide range of incomes. Clearly, these patterns pose a challenge to any simple theory that argues that poverty causes social problems, or that character flaws cause social problems and poverty.

Next, Wilkinson and Pickett looked at the data in a different way. Instead of plotting the social problems index against average income, they plotted it against income inequality. Inequality was measured by taking the share of income going to the richest 20 percent of each country and dividing by the share going to the poorest 20 percent. For the most equal countries, like Sweden and Japan, that ratio is about 4, meaning that the richest fifth of the country makes four times as much as the poorest fifth. For the most unequal countries, like the United States and Portugal, the ratio is around 8.

When you examine the data from this perspective, shown in Figure 2.3, the countries snap crisply into order. Sweden, Japan, and Norway are no longer a hodgepodge of data points but huddle together tightly at the bottom left, with the lowest inequality and the lowest level of health and social problems. Each step you take along the road of inequality toward Finland, Denmark, Belgium, and beyond, you take a step up the ladder of the social problems index. By the time you reach the most unequal nations—the United Kingdom, Portugal, and the United States—they, too,

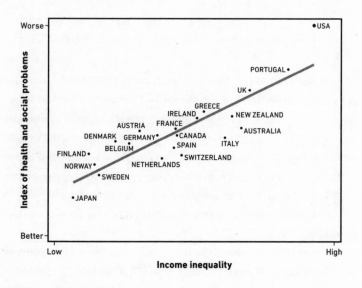

Figure 2.3. Index of health and social problems is strongly associated with income inequality in developed nations. Adapted from Wilkinson and Pickett (2009).

are no longer outliers but fall right along the line where you would expect to find them based on their level of inequality. The correlation with inequality was strong for every one of the ten topics that made up the index, and those links remained intact even when the researchers statistically controlled for each country's average income.

Perhaps the cultures, economies, and governments of these nations are too different to make direct comparisons among them. Wilkinson and Pickett addressed this concern by making the same comparisons across America's fifty states, seen in Figure 2.4. Again, it was the more unequal places that had higher rates of problems, and, again, the effect of inequality was greater than the effect of average income. This explains why rich states, like California, are

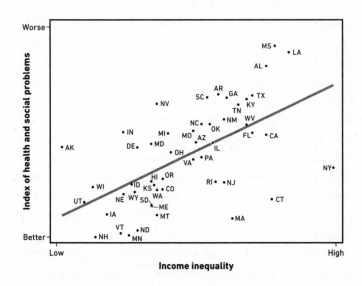

Figure 2.4. Index of health and social problems is strongly associated with income inequality in the United States. Adapted from Wilkinson and Pickett (2009).

clustered in the same area as poor states, like Alabama, and why poor states, like Iowa and Utah, are grouped with rich states, like New Hampshire. Even within a single country, inequality trumps income.

We normally think of the issues that make up the "index of health and social problems" as a function of poverty. But these effects of inequality are consistent after we adjust for income. So, for a person with an average income, living in a more unequal region still puts him at greater risk for life problems. In other words, a middle-class individual in high-inequality Texas will tend to suffer more health and social ills than a middle-class individual in low-inequality Iowa.

Imagine that you are relocating and want to choose a favorable place to live. Most people would choose a neighborhood with low crime rates, good schools, and trustworthy neighbors. One way to identify such places is to do extensive digital reconnaissance, searching online for such data as school test scores and crime statistics. A more effective method would be to look up the Gini coefficient, a measure of economic inequality. Gini statistics are available online for most metropolitan areas. It is fascinating to see how the numbers map onto the actual atmosphere of a particular place. We all have a good sense of what poverty and wealth look and feel like, whether the manicured lawns and sprawling houses of wealthy suburbs, the dilapidated storefronts and potholed streets of a faded city neighborhood, or the rusted house trailers and abandoned appliances that stain the impoverished countryside.

Inequality is harder to see. Places of great inequality have both the manicured lawns and the abandoned storefronts, often separated by only a few blocks. There is no single image in our minds that represents inequality, because its essence is the lack of a single shared experience. In practice, that means a lack of shared spaces, as the haves and the have-nots separate themselves from one another where they live, where they work, and where they go to school.

I moved to North Carolina from Columbus, Ohio. When my wife and I came down to look at places to live, we started with Durham. The first thing we noticed was that the city had millions of trees that covered everything in a leafy canopy that left it shady in the day and pitch black at night. Roads and yards seemed to be carved temporarily out of a thick forest that was waiting to reclaim them at the first chance. Even more striking than its beautiful trees, though, were its extremes.

Driving through Durham, we passed through a neighborhood of million-dollar homes built in the 1920s that had been kept in pristine condition. Magnolias and lemon trees dotted the lawns. Then we crossed one street and suddenly the gorgeous homes were gone. We found ourselves alongside a brick apartment building whose front was covered with the dull metal rungs of fire escapes. Laundry hung in the windows, and on the street men were working on cars. A few blocks farther and we were surrounded by glass office buildings, mixed in with quaint redbrick buildings that had once been tobacco warehouses but had long since been turned into loft apartments with exposed brick and wooden beams. A few blocks on, and chain-link fences topped with razor wire appeared alongside the street. Young men were hanging around on street corners, next to a community center that had posted signs giving notice not to loiter on street corners.

Durham has relatively high crime rates for the area. Its public schools struggle with low test scores and high dropout rates. I assumed that Durham was a poor city. But, in fact, its average income is slightly higher than that of Columbus. What differentiates the two cities is that economic inequality is much higher in Durham. It is home to more poor people, but also to more millionaires.

Columbus has neither of these extremes. Yes, some areas are nicer than others, but it does not leave you with a sense of whiplash, as if you were leaping between cities and possibly centuries within the course of only a few streets.

We stayed in a bed-and-breakfast in a historic neighborhood in Durham while we looked at rental ads. The owners were a friendly married couple who had lived in the city for years. They were proud of their house, which they had lovingly restored. In his day job, the husband was a Durham police officer. Because he knew the city well in a professional capacity, we asked his opinions about the places we were considering. He had strong opinions, and for many of the addresses he would say, "You don't want to live there," or, after a thoughtful pause, "You might be okay there." It was unnerving to hear how wary he was. I asked the innkeeper about one last address. I was sure he would be enthusiastic about it, because it was practically around the corner from his lovely home. He looked at us for a long time before saying anything. Then he said, "Your key will let you in the front or the back door, but the front door is better lighted at night. If you go out after dark, be sure to lock up."

I didn't understand at the time that inequality affects not just the poor, but the whole range of people living in areas beset by it. From an economist's point of view, poverty is very different from economic inequality. Poverty concerns what a person has or lacks, while inequality describes how money is distributed, charting the distance between the haves and have-nots. From a psychological point of view, however, poverty and inequality are intertwined. We perceive our own wealth by comparison to the context, because we perceive virtually everything relative to the context. Our relentless social comparing means that our own worth is never truly separate from that of the haves and have-nots around us. When the rich get richer, everyone else feels poorer. That tendency helps explain why places with high inequality, where stately homes and luxury cars butt up against desolate streets, somehow increase the squalor in everyone's lives. The "somehow" is the subject of the next chapter, in which we will begin to see how inequality changes the ways people think and act.

Chapter 3

Poor Logic

Inequality Has a Logic of Its Own

Jason grew up in one of thirteen A-frame houses along Highway 60 in Maceo, Kentucky. Across the highway lay railroad tracks, where freight trains would thunder through at all hours of the day and night. On the other side of the tracks was an open field that lay fallow throughout the year. It served as a buffer, separating the rails and the road and the houses from a shooting range, where men shot clay pigeons with buckshot. They were far enough from the small neighborhood that you couldn't hear the command to "pull," but only the sound of the guns.

As a kid Jason worked tobacco, chopping the tall stalks and spiking them on long wooden rods until they hung like a curtain of tropical leaves. The sheaves would be passed up through the rafters of the curing barn from one pair of hands to the next, where they would hang to dry through the fall, the barns steaming for months in the fields. Jason had the coveted spot at the top of the rafters. There was greater danger of falling, but the load was lighter because you didn't have to lift the tobacco over your head. It was hard work, but the tobacco tar blackening his hands provided a constant hum of energy as the nicotine leached through skin.

When he was a young man, Jason turned to work in auto body shops, grinding away rust, hammering out dents, and sanding putty into the smooth curves of fenders and hoods. The sandpaper filled his nose with dust and left his hands bleeding at the end of the day. But the job paid better than tobacco. After years of working in other men's shops, he borrowed $80,000 to build his own, eager to escape the limits of an hourly wage. When the shop later went under, he was left deep in debt.

Because he had been purchasing industrial solvents for his business, it was relatively simple to buy other restricted chemicals—chemicals like anhydrous ammonia, used to fertilize fields, kill mold—and to make methamphetamine. After all those years of rust, dust, and tar, here was a way that seemed so much easier. For the first time he had a nice truck and a computer, and could buy his family the clothes and gadgets they had gone without. When he started using the meth himself, he became so full of energy that anything seemed possible. But one night in an anonymous storage shed, a canister of anhydrous ammonia leaked, releasing a noxious odor that led a neighbor to call the police. Jason spent his fortieth birthday in prison. When he walked free after eight years, he had less to show for his hard work than on the day he first set foot in the tobacco field.

Most people think that selling drugs is a way to get rich quick. Why else would they take risks like going to jail, losing everything, or even getting killed? Sociologist Sudhir Venkatesh studied the economics of the drug trade by living with a drug-selling street gang in the dilapidated housing projects of inner-city Chicago. Over the course of several years he not only saw firsthand how the drug trade worked, but also got access to their books to see how the business model worked.

The average drug dealer made about $3.50 an hour, about the same as the minimum wage at that time in the early 1990s. Many of the low-level gang members had second jobs in fast-food restaurants. One level up the chain of command were midlevel gang leaders like J.T., who became Venkatesh's closest informant. J.T. made about $30,000 a year and lived with his mother. For all the participants in the Chicago drug trade, the death rate was astronomically high, driven mostly by gang violence as they competed for turf. Seven percent of the gang members were killed each year, on average. That is many times higher than the mortality rate among U.S. soldiers serving in the wars in Iraq and Afghanistan.

One day over breakfast in a diner, J.T. offered Venkatesh a quiz about how to think like a gangster:

> "Let's say two guys are offering me a great deal on raw product." I knew enough to know that "raw product" meant powdered cocaine, which J.T.'s gang cooked up into crack. "One of them says if I pay twenty percent higher than the usual rate, he'll give me a ten percent discount a year from now, meaning that if the supply goes down, he'll sell to me before the other niggers he deals with. The other guy says he'll give me a ten percent discount now if I agree to buy from him at the regular price a year from now. What would you do? . . ."
>
> "Well, I don't have any idea how this market works, so I'm not sure what to do."
>
> "No, that's not how you need to think. You always take the sure bet in this game. *Nothing* can be predicted—not supply, not anything. The nigger who tells you he's going to have product a year from now is lying. He could be in jail or dead. So take your discount now."

Whether they live in a depressed farm town or an inner-city ghetto, the fate of individuals like Jason and J.T. is familiar. A kid growing up in these environments is many times more likely to end up in prison, drop out of school, or be unemployed than a kid from a middle-class suburb. But where you choose to attribute cause and effect in the stories of these individuals reveals a lot about how you see the world. Many will see young men like Jason and J.T. as responsible for their own problems. Others will focus on their lack of opportunity, due to factors like poverty or poor schools.

If you are like most people, you have given these explanations some thought now and then, and a few of them probably seem pretty convincing. One argument is that some individuals are simply lazy, irresponsible, or unintelligent. In a meritocracy where success is determined by hard work, responsibility, and talent, people who have these character flaws are more likely to commit crimes because of the same moral failings that lead them to be poor in the first place. Their children do worse in school because indolent or negligent parents are less likely to teach their kids good habits, and because intelligence is partially hereditary. Poor teens have unintended pregnancies because they are reckless. And those who lack character are more likely to make bad health decisions like smoking, abusing drugs, and eating too much.

Another version of this theory is that the poor have a different culture, one that does not foster the "middle-class values" of hard work, accountability, and self-reliance. Whether you trace the source of the problem to the individual or the culture, though, the argument is fundamentally the same: Bad character causes poverty and the problems that accompany it.

The character flaw theory is seductive, because it fits in the well-worn groove of how our minds ordinarily search for causes. When we try to understand the reasons for someone's behavior, our intuitive psychology looks first for something in the individual himself. This makes sense as a rule of thumb, because actions often are guided by beliefs, intentions, abilities, and so on. And surely there is some truth to the character flaw theory, given that a brilliant person with an iron will is more likely to succeed than someone with low intelligence and poor self-control.

We take this argument too far, though, when we do not take

into account the fact that actions are also shaped by particular situations. Take, for example, a classic experiment led by psychologist Ned Jones. Research participants heard a speech by a student about his attitude toward Fidel Castro. Half of the time it was a pro-Castro speech, and the other half it was anti-Castro. Half the participants were told that the speaker was free to take any position he wanted, while the other half were told that the researchers had assigned the speaker to advocate for a particular position. After listening to the speech, participants were asked how pro-Castro the speaker's beliefs really were.

The researchers made the very reasonable prediction that when the position in the speech was freely chosen, the audience would believe that the speech would reflect the true attitudes of the speaker, but when the position was assigned, it would assume the speaker had no genuine conviction about the topic. But that very reasonable prediction was wrong: Participants assumed that the speaker actually believed what he said both when the topic of the speech was freely chosen and when it was assigned. In other words, people seemed unable to take the situation into account, instead attributing the speech to the speaker's beliefs even when that assumption flew in the face of logic. We are powerfully biased to look through the specifics of a given situation as if they were a pane of glass and to explain behavior based on the characteristics of a person. This bias has been replicated so many times that researchers took to calling it the "fundamental attribution error."

The fundamental attribution error applies in lots of contexts. The college graduate is smart. The drug addict is weak willed. The person shopping with food stamps is lazy. One reason it is so prevalent is that it is simply easier to think about people than situations. Later studies found that the tendency to neglect the situation was worse when people were distracted by doing a second task at the same time as they made their judgments. In other words, you are more likely to be blind to other people's situations when you are rushed, busy, under-rested, or overburdened. It takes a little extra mental work to consider that the college graduate might have been helped by family connections, or the food stamp recipient might be hardworking and yet stuck in a low-wage job.

Unlike the character flaw theory, another common explanation for self-defeating behavior does take the situation into account. This theory argues that it is poverty itself that causes these life problems. The poor are more likely to commit crimes because they lack more legitimate prospects to earn a living. Poor children do badly in school because schools in poor areas have less money to hire top teachers and their parents have less time to spend helping them with homework. The lack of steady, well-paying jobs means that couples are less likely to marry and form stable families. And poor people have more health issues because they lack nutritious food and access to good medical care. The poor are ultimately no different in their values or behaviors than the middle class. In short, poor environments cause poor outcomes, as a lack of resources leads to a lack of opportunity.

The same stock explanations that we typically hear from pundits are echoed in much of the social science research on inequality, which usually consists of well-meaning, affluent academics trying to explain the problems or symptoms of the poor. I find that these analyses are seriously limited. Both are partly right, and both are partly wrong. The character flaw versus impoverished environment theories are essentially a version of the old nature (character flaws) versus nurture (environment) debate. Like any nature versus nurture discussion, it misses the larger point: Nature and nurture always work together, because what we have inherited genetically as humans is not a rigid set of behaviors, like those that send fruit flies fluttering toward a light.

They are, rather, tendencies to react to changes in the environment in particular ways. The goal should be to comprehend how human nature has prepared us to respond in resource-rich and resource-poor environments, and to high and low levels of inequality. Once we do, we will understand why an individual brought up in a wealthy family would think and act differently than she would if she had been brought up in a poor family, and why an individual living in a situation of great inequality would behave differently than one living in conditions of equality. In that way we will begin to recognize how inequality changes who we are.

The thinking behind the environmental explanation is well intentioned. It avoids blaming the victims of poverty, discrimination, and bad circumstances by focusing on their lack of resources and opportunity as the causal factors. But in doing so, it naively assumes that the decisions and behaviors of the poor are essentially the same as those of the middle class. But as anyone who has lived in both poverty and affluence can attest, people *do* think and act differently in those very different worlds. One difference is how they consider the future.

When I was a child, I would spend most Saturdays playing at my friend Stephen's house. Stephen's family was college educated and solidly middle class. His mother was an insurance agent and his father was a police officer. They were wonderful people, but some of their behaviors befuddled me. For example, Stephen's mom would say, "It's a beautiful day today. What do you two have planned?" It was Saturday, after all, and she expected that we would have an itinerary laid out. We might have said, "Basketball from ten to noon, then a frozen burrito and SunnyD for lunch, and off to play video games until dark," had we been planning at all, but of course we weren't. Or at least, I wasn't. Then one day I was horrified to realize that Stephen *was* secretly planning our schedules. To me, all that preparation seemed uptight, preppy, and somehow feminine. Men, in my world, lived for the present.

This now-bias and the near-pathological aversion to uptightness has gotten me into plenty of trouble over the years. I had to struggle, as I entered college and professional life, to attain the kind of conscientiousness and organization that seemed to come naturally to my middle-class classmates. By my third year of graduate school, I gave up and finally bought a day planner. I now recognize this extreme presentism as a common experience of people who grow up poor.

Of course, this approach to life seems self-defeating. If you want to get out of poverty, you would do well to plan for the future, save money, and invest in the miracle of compound interest. But that's not how people raised in poverty think about the future. The reasons for their perspective are far removed from the kinds of explanations offered by policy wonks and pundits on the nightly news. To understand them, we have to travel thousands of miles and tens of thousands of years to examine how evolution has prepared us to deal with scarce resources.

Live Fast, Die Young

Imagine you are an early human dwelling in the African grasslands. If you are a man, you spend your days hunting and fishing. If your band is in conflict with another band, you are constantly on the watch for enemies, because a raid might happen at any moment. If you are a woman, you are busy gathering fruits and nuts, as your parents did and their parents before them. If you are a young adult, you spend a fair amount of time flirting with other young adults and spreading the gossip that inevitably makes the rounds in a small band where everyone knows everyone else.

Given these conditions, how should you best spend your time and energy?

When we think about that question, we naturally consider what would make us the happiest. But from an evolutionary perspective, we have to remember that nature does not care if we are happy. In fact, nature does not care if we pass on our genes or not. It has no vested interest in whether your family line dies out, or if the whole human species goes extinct. Nature does not advocate for any particular outcome or any particular individual or group. Nature is simply whatever happens.

Still, nature is not merely random, because some behaviors do result in more copies of genes being passed on to future generations than others. Such successful behaviors will tend to be more common in future generations. The rhythm of this creative destruction creates exquisite patterns across the waves of evolutionary time. So to understand human nature from an evolutionary perspective, we have to understand what kinds of behaviors pass on more genes, and in what kinds of environments.

From an evolutionary standpoint, there are only two ways to expend resources that matter: survival and reproduction. Every organism faces a trade-off when it comes to how to invest energy (that is, cellular and metabolic energy, not effort and concentration). On the one hand, it can devote lots of energy to keeping itself alive. To do so, it might build muscle for strength and the immune system for maintaining health. On the other hand, it can allocate its energy to reproduction, creating eggs and sperm and the whole system of hormones and the sexy adult bodies that get eggs and sperm introduced to each other. Of course, we don't control that trade-off with conscious choices. But various physiological systems in our bodies are constantly regulating how much energy we are spending on these various construction projects (as we will see in more detail in the chapter on stress and health).

Which investment—the survival of our bodies or the creation of new ones—offers the best chance to pass along one's genes? It depends. Among other things, it depends on whether times are good or bad. When times are prosperous and the future looks secure, it is a sign that you are likely to live a long and healthy life. You will leave more descendants if you bide your time and wait to have children until you are really ready to support them well. You should devote everything you can to extensive parenting to make sure that they survive to reproduce themselves, and maybe you can even help raise your grandchildren.

When times are hard, the future is uncertain, and enemies are lurking behind every patch of grass, the odds favor an entirely different approach. You might not live long enough to have children later. Under those conditions, it pays to reproduce early and often. If you are going to reproduce at all, the best bet is to do so as soon as possible. The first approach is what evolutionary biologists call a "slow strategy" of investing for the future. The second is a "fast strategy," as in, "live fast, die young."

Of course, early *Homo sapiens* did not adopt a conscious strategy about how to maximize their genetic fitness. In our early history, however, those who took the fast approach when times were difficult and the slow approach when times were favorable left more descendants than those who were less responsive to the environment. As a result, there were more people in the next generation inclined to toggle between fast strategies in hard times and slow strategies in good ones. Now, so many generations later, we are the descendants of ancestors who were very, very good at adopting these tactics.

Biologists have known for decades that animals adapt to changes in their environments by shifting along the fast-slow continuum. They observed, for example, that butterflies that lived in locations that had a lot of predators would reproduce earlier, devoting less metabolic energy to growth and more to reproduction. The same species in a location with few predators would live longer and would therefore take the opposite approach, starting reproduction later. The definitive evidence came, however, when scientists started doing experiments in the lab to ensure that it really was the dangerous conditions that caused the adaptations.

In one study biologists bred a population of about eight hundred fruit flies from ten "Adams" and ten "Eves." Then they divided them up into two genetically identical groups. One was fortunate enough to be in the Safe group, which lived out its days eating, reproducing, and doing whatever fruit flies do for fun. The other group was not as lucky. Twice a week 90 percent of this Die Young group was killed and replaced with new flies. The researchers continued this process for four years.

Reading the scientific report of this experiment is unnerving. You can't help but imagine the situation from the perspective of the flies, finding yourself in this sci-fi nightmare in which some crazed giants in lab coats keep "disappearing" everyone you know. The experimental condition is euphemistically described as the "HAM [high adult mortality] treatment," and mortality rate is precisely quantified: "The probability of surviving 1 week as an adult was $P = 0.01$."

Despite its violence, the study reported important results. The flies in the Die Young group started reproducing at an earlier age, and they laid more eggs per female than those in the Safe group. This is just the effect predicted by the live fast, die young theory. It was not that the flies looked around, decided it was getting dangerous, and made a decision to start a family sooner. The flies that were able to reproduce early simply left more descendants in future generations.

In 1991 psychologist Jay Belsky and colleagues made an argument, based on the evolutionary fast-slow trade-off, that women raised in harsh, stressful, or chaotic environments would be more likely to have children earlier. There was not much data available, however, to test his theory at the time. A few years later, psychologists Margo Wilson and Martin Daly took up the challenge by studying birth and death rates in Chicago. Chicago is a city of neighborhoods. You might start in Lincoln Park, with its leafy streets, wrought-iron streetlamps, and redbrick brownstones. If you travel south to Englewood, with its barren concrete, windowless buildings, and sidewalks strewn with broken glass, you would be forgiven for thinking that in twelve short miles you had crossed some invisible border into another country. In some ways, you have.

Wilson and Daly looked at the average age at which women had their first child in each of Chicago's neighborhoods. As predicted, women gave birth earlier in poorer areas. They then correlated the age at first birth with life expectancies in each neighborhood, because from an evolutionary perspective it is life expectancy that is the most important source of pressure for reproducing earlier. The correlation was strikingly large, almost a one-to-one correspondence: As life expectancy decreased, so did the women's age when they started having children. Just as the live fast, die young theory predicts, when people die young, they give birth sooner.

In the years since that groundbreaking research, dozens of studies have confirmed Wilson and Daly's results. Women brought up in poor or dangerous environments have children earlier. They also have more children, on average, which is another way to increase the chances of passing on genes.

The theory proposed by Belsky therefore seems to have been borne out by the data. But Belsky had not only predicted earlier births. He went further, arguing that the "strategy" for women raised in adversity to have children earlier and more frequently was not simply a choice. Rather, it was a response to the amount of certainty or uncertainty in their environment, which should affect the way they related to the world and to other people, both mentally and physically. Belsky had predicted that girls raised in poor, dangerous, or chaotic conditions would actually reach puberty and begin menstruating earlier than those raised in stable middle-class homes. If so, they would begin having children sooner, on average, because of their earlier maturation. This was a bolder prediction, because it suggested that home conditions not only affected people's choices, but also their biology.

This work set off a flurry of studies in the 1990s in which researchers from many different labs tracked families for years, from the time that new babies were born through the time when they began having children of their own. If it really was the chaotic environment that caused the changes in birth rates, then the age at which girls reached puberty should be predictable even before they were born, knowing nothing about them other than their neighborhood or family situation. In study after study, Belsky's prediction was confirmed. By the mid-2000s, it was clear that girls raised in harsh, poor, or chaotic homes reached puberty earlier than those raised in more stable homes.

These results also pushed the theory further in another way. Although the animal studies focused on death rates and birth rates, the human studies looked at a much broader range of troubles. Earlier puberty and earlier childbirth were linked not only to life expectancies, but also to poverty, to homes with an absent father, and to the degree of economic inequality in the region. Even though these sorts of hardships are not themselves lethal (at least not directly), they seemed to cue the same kinds of biological and psychological changes as high mortality rates do.

How extensive are the effects of the fast-slow trade-off among humans? Psychology experiments suggest that they are much more prevalent than anyone previously suspected, influencing people's behaviors and decisions in ways that have nothing to do with reproduction. Some of the most important now versus later trade-offs involve money. Financial advisers tell us that if we skip our daily latte and instead save that three dollars a day, we could increase our savings by more than a thousand dollars a year. But that means facing a daily choice: How much do I want a thousand dollars in the bank at the end of the year? And how great would a latte taste right now?

The same evaluations lurk behind larger life decisions. Do I invest time and money in going to college, hoping for a higher salary in the long run, or do I take a job that guarantees an income now? Do I work at a regular job and play by the rules, even if I will probably struggle financially all my life, or do I sell drugs? If I choose drugs, I might lose everything in the long run and end up broke, in jail, or dead. But I might make a lot of money today.

Even short-term feelings of affluence or poverty can make people more or less shortsighted. Recall from the earlier chapters that subjective sensations of poverty and plenty have powerful effects, and those are usually based on how we measure ourselves against other people. Psychologist Mitch Callan and colleagues combined these two principles and predicted that when people are made to feel poor, they will become myopic, taking whatever they can get immediately and ignoring the future. When they are made to feel rich, they would take the long view.

Their study began by asking research participants a long series of probing questions about their finances, their spending habits, and even their personality traits and personal tastes. They told participants that they needed all this detailed information because their computer program was going to calculate a personalized "Comparative Discretionary Income Index." They were informed that the computer would give them a score that indicated how much money they had compared with other people who were similar to them in age, education level, personality traits, and so on. In reality, the computer program did none of that, but merely displayed a little flashing progress bar and the words

"Calculating. Please wait . . ." Then it provided random feedback to participants, telling half that they had more money than most people like them, and the other half that they had less money than other people like them.

Next, participants were asked to make some financial decisions, and were offered a series of choices that would give them either smaller rewards received sooner or larger rewards received later. For example, they might be asked, "Would you rather have $100 today or $120 next week? How about $100 today or $150 next week?" After they answered many such questions, the researchers could calculate how much value participants placed on immediate rewards, and how much they were willing to wait for a better long-term payoff.

The study found that, when people felt poor, they tilted to the fast end of the fast-slow trade-off, preferring immediate gratification. But when they felt relatively rich, they took the long view. To underscore the point that this was not simply some abstract decision without consequences in the real world, the researchers performed the study again with a second group of participants. This time, instead of hypothetical choices, the participants were given twenty dollars and offered the chance to gamble with it. They could decline, pocket the money, and go home, or they could play a card game against the computer and take their chances, in which case they either would lose everything or might make much more money. When participants were made to feel relatively rich, 60 percent chose to gamble. When they were made to feel poor, the number rose to 88 percent. Feeling poor made people more willing to roll the dice.

The astonishing thing about these experiments was that it did not take an entire childhood spent in poverty or affluence to change people's level of shortsightedness. Even the mere subjective feeling of being less well-off than others was sufficient to trigger the live fast, die young approach to life.

Nothing to Lose

Most of the drug-dealing gang members that Sudhir Venkatesh followed were earning the equivalent of minimum wage and living with their mothers. If they weren't getting rich and the job was so dangerous, then why did they choose to do it? Because there were a few top gang members who were making several hundred thousand dollars a year. They made their wealth conspicuous by driving luxury cars and wearing expensive clothes and flashy jewelry. They traveled with entourages. The rank-and-file gang members did not look at one another's lives and conclude that this was a terrible job. They looked instead at the top and imagined what they could be. Despite the fact that their odds of success were impossibly low, even the slim chance of making it big drove them to take outrageous risks.

The live fast, die young theory explains why people would focus on the here and now and neglect the future when conditions make them feel poor. But it does not tell the whole story. The research described in Chapter 2 revealed that rates of many health and social problems were higher, even among members of the middle class, in societies where there was more inequality. One of the puzzling aspects of the rapid rise of inequality over the past three decades is that almost all of the change in fortune has taken place at the top. The incomes of the poor and the middle class are not too different from where they were in 1980, once the numbers are adjusted for inflation. But the income and wealth of the top 1 percent have soared, and those of the top one tenth of a percent dwarfed even their increases. How are the gains of the superrich having harmful effects on the health and well-being of the rest of us?

Part of the answer to that question can be found within the hives of bumblebees. Ecologist Ralph Cartar was studying the feeding habits of wild bumblebees on a little island off the coast of British Columbia. Bees there fed on the nectar mainly from two types of flowers: seablush and dwarf huckleberry. Seablush is a tall flower topped with bursts of bright pink petals. A field of seablush looks like an impressionist painting, a thousand points of pink against the green of summer. Dwarf huckleberry is a humbler plant with the appearance of a wild bush, bearing perhaps only a few blue berries and a few tiny flowers hanging downward like white bells. A field of dwarf huckleberry could be mistaken for a meadow of weeds.

Cartar noticed that seablush and dwarf huckleberry are judged very differently from the bees' point of view. The insects get about the same amount of nutrition from either kind of flower on average. But opting for seablush guarantees a sure thing. If they go to have a drink in the field of seablush, they will never leave thirsty, for each flower has about the same modest amount of nectar—which means they will never strike it rich, either. Seablush is therefore a low-risk, low-reward investment. Dwarf huckleberry, in contrast, is bumblebee blackjack: Some flowers contain a jackpot of nectar, while others have none. Dwarf huckleberry is a high-risk, high-reward gamble.

Cartar set out to test an evolutionary theory about risk taking, which I'll call the "nothing to lose theory." It says that for any foraging organism, from bumblebees to hunter-gatherers, the amount of risk it is willing to take depends on how needy it is. A well-fed bumblebee can afford to play it safe and stick to the seablush. But consider a bee that is close to starvation, unlikely to survive on the meager nectar from the seablush flower. That desperate bee, with nothing to lose, will take its chances and light out in search of a windfall among the dwarf huckleberry. That is to say, as needs increase, so, too, does risk taking.

To test this theory, Cartar had to compare the foraging choices of the bees when they were well fed and when they were needy. Each day he and his assistants visited fourteen bee colonies. On some days they would steal the nectar in certain nests, siphoning it out through little tubes, and then give it to other nests. The following day they would reverse the procedure, so that the nests that had been robbed the previous day were now given bonus nectar. The researchers would then count how many bees from each colony went to each flower patch each day. (The bees were marked with different colors to identify their home colonies.) As Cartar suspected, when the bees received bonus nectar, they played it safe and fed in the seablush fields. But when their nectar was removed, they headed straight for the dwarf huckleberry fields.

Calculating the best option in an uncertain environment is a complicated matter; even humans have a hard time with it. According to traditional economic theories, rational decision making means maximizing your payoffs. You can calculate your "expected utility" by multiplying the size of the reward by the likelihood of getting it. So, an option that gives you a 90 percent chance of winning $500 has a greater expected utility than an option that gives you a 40 percent chance of winning $1,000 ($500 × .90 = $450 as compared with $1,000 × .40 = $400). But the kind of decision making demonstrated by the bumblebees doesn't necessarily line up well with the expected utility model. Neither, it turns out, do the risky decisions made by the many other species that also show the same tendency to take big risks when they are needy.

Humans are one of those species. Imagine what you would do if you owed a thousand dollars in rent that was due today or you would lose your home. In a gamble, would you take the 90 percent chance of winning $500, or the 40 percent chance of winning $1,000? Most people would opt for the smaller chance of getting the $1,000, because if they won, their need would be met.

Although it is irrational from the expected utility perspective, it is rational in another sense, because meeting basic needs is sometimes more important than the mathematically best deal. The fact that we see the same pattern across animal species suggests that evolution has found need-based decision making to be adaptive, too. From the humble bumblebee, with its tiny brain, to people trying to make ends meet, we do not always seek to maximize our profits. Call it Mick Jagger logic: If we can't always get what we want, we try to get what we need. Sometimes that means taking huge risks.

We saw in Chapter 2 that people judge what they need by making comparisons to others, and the impact of comparing to those at the top is much larger than comparing to those at the bottom. If rising inequality makes people feel that they need more, and higher levels of need lead to risky choices, it implies a fundamentally new relationship between inequality and risk: Regardless of whether you are poor or middle class, inequality itself might cause you to engage in riskier behavior.

To test whether inequality actually increases risk taking, my collaborators and I designed a simple experiment. Participants in the study were asked to make a series of gambling decisions. Each one offered a range of choices from low risk/low reward options (say, a 100 percent chance of winning 15 cents) to high risk/high reward options (such as a 10 percent chance of winning $1.50). They were divided into two groups, and before they gambled, we provided them with information about how previous players had done, which was the crucial experimental factor. In the Equal group, participants were told that the top performers earned only a few cents more than the lowest-performing group. In the Unequal group, they were told that the top performers earned dramatically more than the low performers, who walked away with almost nothing. The average earnings in both experimental conditions were the same. After participants were told how previous players had done, they indicated how much money they would need to be satisfied in the game, and then they played the game themselves.

As we expected, players in the Unequal group indicated that they would need much more money to be satisfied than those in the Equal group. In a situation where there is a great deal of inequality, players felt needier. As a result, when the Unequal group made gambling decisions themselves, they took more risks, preferring high risk/high reward choices. The critical factor in this experiment was that the two groups, whose members had similar average incomes and education levels, did not start off with different amounts of money. They had not yet played the game, so they had no winnings to worry about losing. Yet simply being aware that there was a big gap between the winners and the losers made the Unequal group take more chances. This experiment provided the first evidence that inequality *itself* can cause risky behavior.

What were the implications? By definition, in the Unequal group a small number of players won bigger rewards, but most of them lost. In the Equal group, fewer people got extremely high payoffs, but fewer people lost everything. In other words, by causing riskier decisions, inequality led to greater differences between the haves and the have-nots. Inequality, in effect, bred even greater inequality.

Experiments like this are a Petri dish for psychologists, who can tightly control a situation and use random assignment, which is essential for getting a clean answer about cause and effect. But in the process of bringing the problem into the lab, they remove it from its everyday context. For our own experiment, we wanted to know whether the same dynamic would hold true in the wild. Is risk taking one of the linchpins connecting inequality to more chaotic lives for ordinary people?

One common way that researchers measure risk taking is

simply to ask participants about their behavior by using surveys. For a lot of the kinds of risks that get people into trouble, though, this technique presents problems. "Thank you for taking our survey, ma'am. Now, how often in the past year have you made foolish financial decisions? How often have you engaged in risky health behaviors, like having unprotected sex? How about drinking and driving? And how often have you ignored the law and dabbled in using or selling illegal drugs?" There are obvious ethical issues involved in asking people to admit doing things that are at best embarrassing and at worst unlawful. Even if you did pose those kinds of questions, it would be hard to trust the answers.

Instead, we used a different method to measure risky behaviors in everyday life. We turned to Google to seek out terms that people might search for if they were engaged in particular kinds of risky behaviors. We began by identifying three areas in which risky decisions might cause real problems: financial decision making, sexual behavior, and the use of drugs and alcohol. Once we had settled on sex, drugs, and money, we asked ourselves: What might I search for if I was engaged in risky behavior of this type?

People googling terms like "lottery tickets" and "payday loans," for example, are probably already involved in some risky spending. To measure sexual riskiness, we counted searches for the morning-after pill and for STD testing. And to measure drug- and alcohol-related risks, we counted searches for how to get rid of a hangover and how to pass a drug test. Of course, a person might search for any of these terms for reasons unrelated to engaging in risky behaviors. But, on average, if there are more people involved in sex, drugs, and money risks, you would expect to find more of these searches.

Armed with billions of such data points from Google, we asked whether the states where people searched most often for those terms were also the states with higher levels of income inequality. To help reduce the impact of idiosyncrasies related to each search term, we averaged the six terms together into a general risk-taking index. Then we plotted that index against the degree of inequality in each state. The states with higher inequality had much higher risk taking, as estimated from their Google searches. This relationship remained strong after statistically adjusting for the average income in each state.

If the index of risky googling tracks real-life risky behavior, then we would expect it to be associated with poor life outcomes. So we took our Google index and tested whether it could explain the link, reported in Chapter 2, between inequality and Richard Wilkinson and Kate Pickett's index of ten major health and social problems. Indeed, the risky googling index was strongly correlated with the index of life problems. Using sophisticated statistical analyses, we found that inequality was a strong predictor of risk taking, which in turn was a strong predictor of health and social problems. These findings suggest that risky behavior is a pathway that helps explain the link between inequality and bad outcomes in everyday life. The evidence becomes much stronger still when we consider these correlations together with the evidence of cause and effect provided by the laboratory experiments.

Experiments like the ones described in this chapter are essential for understanding the effects of inequality, because only experiments can separate the effects of the environment from individual differences in character traits. Surely there were some brilliant luminaries and some dullards in each experimental group. Surely there were some hearty souls endowed with great self-control, and some irresponsible slackers, too. Because they were assigned to the experimental groups at random, it is exceedingly unlikely that the groups differed consistently in their personalities or abilities. Instead, we can be confident that the differences we see are caused by the experimental factor, in this case making decisions in a context of high or low inequality.

John Bradford was a sixteenth-century Protestant theologian who rose to prominence under King Edward VI. His fate changed swiftly when Edward died and Queen Mary Tudor ascended the throne. A Catholic, she was called "Bloody Mary" for the hundreds of Protestants she burned at the stake. Imprisoned in the Tower of London, Bradford watched as other prisoners were led down the hall to their execution. For most of that time he did not know whether he would be released or executed. He would remark to his cellmates that what separated his fate from that of the doomed was nothing in his power, nothing he could predict, nothing his brilliance could change. Experiments are gentle reminders that, in the words of John Bradford, "There but for the grace of God go I." If we deeply understand behavioral experiments, they make us humble. They challenge our assumption that we are always in control of our own successes and failures. They remind us that, like John Bradford, we are not simply the products of our thoughts, our plans, or our bootstraps.

These experiments suggest that any average person, thrust into these different situations, will start behaving differently. Imagine that you are an evil scientist with a giant research budget and no ethical review board. You decide to take ten thousand newborn babies and randomly assign them to be raised by families in a variety of places. You place some with affluent, well-educated parents in the suburbs of Atlanta. You place others with single mothers in inner-city Milwaukee, and so on. The studies we've looked at suggest that the environments you assign them to will have major effects on their futures. The children you assign to highly unequal places, like Texas, will have poorer outcomes than those you assign to more equal places, like Iowa, even though Texas and Iowa have about the same average income.

In part, this will occur because bad things are more likely to happen to them in unequal places. And in part, it will occur because the children raised in unequal places will behave differently. All of this can transpire even though the babies you are randomly assigning begin life with the same potential abilities and values.

The results of our experiments on inequality and risk taking made me think again of Jason, who is not just another subject in my studies. He is my older brother. I worked tobacco, too, and felt the cutaneous buzz of tobacco tar. I worked for him in his body shop, sanding primer until my fingerprints had evaporated on hot summer days. One summer day when I was in high school, when Jason still had his body shop, he stopped by our parents' house and asked me if I wanted to take a ride with him to Frankfort. He was selling a car that he had bought cheap and restored, and had to pick up the original title in the state capital. He was being kind to get a bored teenager out of the house but also wanted company for the drive, two and a half hours each way. Speeding down the highway in his truck, we talked more seriously than we normally would have. I got the sense that something was on his mind.

The traffic ahead of us slowed and then came to a standstill. Staring at the trail of red brake lights ahead, Jason suddenly turned the wheel to the left, and we drove off the road, down into the grassy median strip that was several times wider than the asphalt lanes on either side. We bobbed back uphill and onto the opposite lane, speeding now in the other direction. We pulled off the highway onto an exit and started driving down small country roads to avoid the jammed traffic. "Be damned if I'm going to wait for that," he explained. A little while later, back on the highway, Jason took out a small carved wooden case. From one side of the mysterious object he pulled a small stainless steel tube. He pushed the tube into the other side of the case, pulling it out again with a small wad of crushed marijuana stuffed into one end. Steering the truck with his knee, he lit the end of the tube with a cigarette lighter. A pipe! I was impressed by the ingenious little device. I supposed that it was more practical than getting out rolling papers while driving.

Back in the quiet drone of the highway, Jason talked about how he had no way of predicting whether his body shop would be there in a year. "I'm never gonna have nothing," he said. "So I gotta do what I'm gonna do now."

Chapter 4

The Right, the Left, and the Ladder

How Inequality Divides Our Politics

It must have been disorienting for the Baron de Gauville, surrounded by the familiar luxury of the palace of Versailles, to find himself so close to chaos. By 1791 France's traditional assembly, the Estates General, had been replaced by one new version of parliament after another, each splintering into bickering factions before collapsing into the next incarnation. King Louis XVI vacillated between persuasion and force as he struggled to remain in possession of his country and, eventually, his head.

As the newest version of parliament met for the first time, the members sorted themselves amid the confusion into groups of like-minded men. De Gauville reported, "We began to recognize each other: those who were loyal to religion and the king took up positions to the right of the [king's] chair so as to avoid the shouts, oaths, and indecencies that enjoyed free rein in the opposing camp." The militant revolutionaries who wanted to overthrow the monarchy, and those who were dedicated to the rational ethos of the Enlightenment rather than the authority of the Church, meanwhile, drifted to the left side. Those with more moderate views occupied the center of the room.

Though unplanned, the seating arrangement was not entirely unpredictable. In the old Estates General, the king had invited the clergy (the first estate) and the nobility (the second estate) to sit at his right, and the working people (the third estate) to take seats at his left. As in many cultures around the world, in the Judeo-Christian tradition favored parties are granted seats on the right. In the Bible, Jesus sits at the right hand of God. In French *gauche* literally means "left," but in English we use the term to mean "inelegant" or "unsophisticated," much like the "shouts, oaths, and indecencies" de Gauville disdained. Similarly, French *à droite* (to the right) became the English "adroit," meaning "skillful" or "talented." By the time de Gauville was describing events of the French Revolution, the king was no longer telling the noblemen where to sit, yet his supporters seemed more comfortable at his right, and his enemies at his left.

In the weeks that followed, writers reporting news of the assembly began referring to the various factions with the shorthand of "the left," "the right," and "the center." "Right" and "left" thus became ensconced in our political vocabulary as descriptions for conservatives and liberals, respectively. If the assembly hall at Versailles had been laid out differently, we might speak today of conservatives as the "front" and liberals as the "rear."

Despite their origins in historical accident, the labels retain some of their original connotation. Is the political right good and the left bad? The question is, good for *whom*? From the perspective of the king, the traditionalists who wanted to preserve the monarchy and the old ways of doing things were good, while those who wanted to change the rules of society were bad. They were indeed good and bad—but only from the point of view of people in command in traditional power structures. That was true in eighteenth-century France, and it is true today.

It is not always obvious why a particular issue lines up with the liberal or conservative perspective. Why should someone who supports a woman's right to have an abortion also want to raise taxes on people with high incomes? Why should the same person who believes in the right to own assault rifles also distrust the scientific findings on climate change? Why would people's attitudes toward illegal immigration be linked with their views on gay marriage?

Political psychologists have proposed a lot of schemes over the years to explain the core ways in which conservatives and liberals differ. Are they the product of strict versus permissive parenting? A function of rigid versus fluid thinking? Religious versus secular worldviews? Psychologist John Jost reviewed the historical perspectives and dozens of empirical studies and found that the left and the right consistently differ from each other in two fundamental ways.

The first and most obvious is that conservatives generally want to preserve tradition and the status quo, while liberals want to see changes in society. This distinction between tradition and change looks different, however, from their respective points of view. Conservatives don't prefer the status quo simply for the sake of keeping things the same. They tend to believe, like the philosopher Thomas Hobbes, that a society in chaos is the worst possible condition. Conservatives are therefore sensitive to threats to social order, be they external (rival armies) or internal (potential revolutionaries). Civil order is difficult to achieve, and conservatives believe we should work to safeguard it. That usually means trusting in traditional ways of doing things that have been tested by time. If that means forgoing some opportunities to improve society by changing its rules, it is a price worth paying.

Similarly, liberals don't want change just for the sake of change, but tend to view some aspects of society as working well and others as working poorly. Established ways of doing things have led to both, so they are not especially impressed with tradition and feel compelled to change the things they think are dysfunctional. They tend to have more confidence than conservatives do in the power of human reason to find rational solutions to problems. Following in the footsteps of philosophers like Jean-Jacques Rousseau and

John Locke, they are motivated to keep rewriting the rules of society in order to keep improving it.

The second fundamental distinction between conservatives and liberals is their willingness to accept inequality. Again, most conservatives do not want inequality for its own sake. Instead, they view it as an outcome of an emphasis on individual rights, abilities, and responsibilities. When individuals outcompete others, the result is always some degree of inequality. Contrary to the perceptions of many liberals, most conservatives aren't animated by the idea of hierarchy itself. They just aren't bothered by it the way liberals are.

Liberals, contrary to the perspective of many conservatives, are not hostile to the idea of individual rights and responsibilities, or market competition. Instead, they see individual merit as just one factor among many that determines success or failure in a competitive market. They tend to consider the economic system as a whole rather than just the individual players within it, which means taking into account such factors as monopolies, old-boy networks, institutional racism and sexism, and cycles of advantage and disadvantage that shape people's outcomes for reasons that have nothing to do with individual virtues. They have no special love of "big government" and are often puzzled by conservatives' apparent obsession with the size of government. Liberals see both government policies and markets as useful, but imperfect, tools for improving society.

Ultimately, life is too complex to assess it from a single point of view. As liberals like to emphasize, we know from statistics and from experience that most people who start out with nothing end up poor, and most people who start off affluent remain so. Nonetheless, as conservatives often point out, individual talent and responsibility can be powerful. Some exceptional individuals are able to transcend poverty and limited opportunity to achieve great success. What is true of a system in general is not

Figure 4.1. A murmuration of starlings.

necessarily true of all the individuals within it. Consider a murmuration of starlings.

Each bird in this marvelously named flock flies according to its own self-interest. By staying within the flock, an individual bird is protected from hawks and other predators. No single bird knows where the flock is heading next, and there is no leader directing the group. Each bird simply watches and listens to others nearby and tries to stay close to them. When ten thousand starlings all follow the same simple rule, the result is an astonishing shadow undulating across the landscape, a wave one moment and a whirlpool the next, then suddenly a spiraling helix, coming apart like a mammoth amoeba, then merging, whole again. As poet Richard Wilbur put it, "What is an individual thing? They roll / Like a drunken fingerprint across the sky!"

When you focus on the swarm as a whole, it appears to be a single organism, and it is difficult to keep track of the individuals within it.

And yet if you focus on the movements of an individual starling, its behavior is not the same as the flock as a whole. At any moment, the bird may be moving forward when the flock is moving left. It may be diving when the column is swirling. Like a visual illusion that registers as a duck one moment and a rabbit the next, it is impossible to see both the individuals and the whole simultaneously.

The same is true of societies and economies: You can focus on the individual or the system, but it's hard to see both at once. Conservatives focus on the individuals within the system. This young man is responsible for getting a job. That young woman should make choices that enable her to avoid being a single mother. If they don't, then they suffer the consequences. Liberals look at the system and perceive that places where poverty is the norm just keep reproducing generations of poverty. Even when kids work hard, few can escape. If you want to predict who gets a job or who becomes a single mother, start by assessing their parents' incomes and the quality of their schools.

We saw in Chapter 3 that both perspectives are oversimplifications, because inequality in the society affects the behaviors of individuals, which leads in turn to greater inequality. Conservatives and liberals generally agree that individual responsibility, talent, and hard work are important factors in achieving success, and they agree that context matters as well. One group's main emphasis, however, is the other's background. When the system is in the spotlight, hierarchy and inequality come sharply into focus. When the individual is in the spotlight, hierarchy and inequality fall where they may.

We have seen that tradition versus change and hierarchy versus equality are two fundamental principles that orient moral compasses. Yet there is no philosophical reason why those who prefer tradition also have to accept hierarchy, or why those who prefer change should also desire equality. Jost and colleagues point out that it is not philosophy that makes these needles align, but history. Since the Enlightenment, many Western societies have gradually become less hierarchical. Monarchies have given way to democracies. Slavery has been abolished. Women and black people have gained the right to vote and became equal, at least in the eyes of the law. In the twenty-first century we have seen equality extended further to gay men and lesbians, transgender individuals, and others. Because of these historical trends, the old power structures that remain tend to be the more hierarchical, while new ones are more equal. A preference for tradition is therefore more likely to be accompanied by a tolerance for inequality, and preferences for change are more open to greater equality.

A fascinating historical exception shows that the link between preferences for traditional power structures and inequality is not inevitable. Psychologist Sam McFarland studied the beliefs of people in Russia in the 1990s. After decades of communist government that was authoritarian and yet promoted relative economic equality, the breakup of the Soviet Union led to dramatic increases in inequality. It was a turbulent time in which capitalist markets took hold with little or no regulation. Economic security for the average person evaporated, while a few well-connected individuals became billionaires. McFarland and his colleagues measured people's opinions about the new economic conditions and the degree of support for the old communist days. They also assessed Russians' preferences for traditional authority and stability over change. In Russia, unlike North America and Western Europe, a respect for tradition was strongly correlated with a desire for greater equality. A longing for the ancien régime can therefore have different meanings, depending on the nature of that regime.

We have been talking about liberals and conservatives as different types of people, and of course, to some extent, they are. But categorizing people by their politics is another way that our stereotypes of people are much more rigid and extreme than the actual people themselves. All of us, from time to time, find ourselves thinking along the lines of "the other party," when the truth is that, politically speaking, we all contain multitudes.

Most days when I am at work, I walk along Franklin Street, Chapel Hill's main strip. On any trip along Franklin to get lunch or a cup of coffee, you can expect to be asked for money by a panhandler. I have been surprised by my own reactions to these overtures. Sometimes I hand over a bit of money; on most days I just say, "Sorry," and keep walking. But more disturbing to me than my inconsistent behavior are my inconsistent thoughts. Some days when I hear, "Spare change?" I look up and I see someone who is having a hard time. I see someone who probably didn't have much opportunity starting out, who had more than his fair share of bad luck, and who needs a little help when he is at his lowest. On other days, I see someone who is so irresponsible that he is lying in the bed that he has made for himself. Someone who might be gainfully employed if he put as much effort into getting up in the morning and going to work as he does into pestering other, working people for their money. Sometimes I have both these reactions in the span of an hour. Why does our stream of consciousness sometimes seem as if it has flipped channels between Paul Krugman and Rush Limbaugh?

Psychologists Aaron Kay and Richard Eibach argue that we each carry around an "ideological toolbox" in our heads. We think of our political beliefs as a stable set of principles supported by a solid foundation of logic and facts. But in fact they are more like an assortment of tools that we choose among depending on the demands of a particular moment. Sometimes the ideological principles we turn to depend on what we have been thinking about lately. If I read a news story about a crime committed by a homeless person a few minutes before my walk down

Franklin Street, I am more likely to think about the next pan-handler I see in negative terms, simply because those ideas have been brought recently to mind. Psychologists call this phenomenon "accessibility." Like Google, the mind keeps recently used ideas at the forefront of consciousness so that we can access them easily at a moment's notice. Accessibility does not follow rules of logical consistency. If I show you the words "ocean" and "moon," then ask you to name a good laundry detergent, you are likely to say, "Tide." It doesn't matter that the laundry detergent is logically unrelated to oceans and moons. Having used an interconnected web of ideas recently, you are more likely to travel along that network in the future.

A second reason that our internal monologues can toggle between liberal and conservative channels is that we do not keep track of the logical consistency of our thoughts the way we believe we do. Psychologists Lars Hall, Petter Johansson, and colleagues showed how flexible our political opinions can be in a striking study of what they call "choice blindness." They surveyed voters in Sweden about a range of controversial issues during a national election campaign. Like the United States, Sweden is firmly divided between liberal and conservative parties. Although both are well to the left of their American counterparts, citizens are evenly distributed between them, with only about 10 percent undecided at the time of the study. The survey asked about twelve divisive issues on which the two parties disagreed—for example, should the gasoline tax be increased? should Sweden restart its nuclear energy program?—and the research subjects indicated their agreement or disagreement with each option. They also indicated how likely they were to vote for each party, how certain they were about their opinions, and how engaged they were in politics.

The survey was delivered to each participant on a clipboard. That might sound like a mundane detail, but it was actually the key to the experimenter's mischievous plan. As each subject filled in his answers, the experimenter watched him and secretly completed another survey that was identical, except for one small detail: The experimenter reversed the subject's answers to half of the questions. When the subject handed over his completed survey, the experimenter took it, made some notes in a notebook, and then handed the clipboard back. But through a magician's sleight of hand, the experimenter handed the subject the reversed survey instead. In a control condition, the original survey was returned to the subjects.

The subjects were then asked to explain why they expressed the opinions they did for each question. During this discussion, they were asked if they wanted to correct or adjust any of their answers before talking about them. Astonishingly, 47 percent of the subjects who received the reversed answers did not notice any changes at all. Of the other 53 percent, most people detected only one or two. Only one person was suspicious that the experimenters had switched his answers. The rest said that they had misread the question or accidentally marked the wrong answer. When they discussed their answers, subjects who failed to observe the switch gave perfectly reasonable arguments for positions they hadn't originally taken.

This is one of those experiments where it is impossible to put yourself in the position of the subjects. We simply can't imagine trying to explain why taxes should be cut when we just said they should be raised, or vice versa. Surely we would never fall for that sort of trickery, and yet nearly half of the people in the study did. Were they just being polite, rather than correcting the experimenter? If so, then accepting the reversed opinions as their own should have no effect on subjects' actual beliefs. To test this idea, the experimenters asked subjects at the end of the study to rate, again, how likely they were to vote for one of the two parties in the upcoming election. In the control condition, the answers were virtually identical to voting intentions expressed at the beginning of the study. But in the reversed condition, subjects shifted their voting intentions significantly in the direction of the reversed answers.

Bizarrely, these shifts were just as strong for those who expressed great certainty in their vote at the start of the survey as for those who were more tentative. The shifts were equivalent for those highly engaged in politics and the disengaged; for liberals and conservatives; for men and women; for young and old. This finding, though striking, is not an anomaly. Hall and Johansson's team has repeated the same sleight-of-hand experiments using many kinds of preferences, from moral principles to attractiveness ratings of photographs to the taste of jam and tea. In every case, a large percentage—typically between 50 percent and 80 percent—fail to notice the switch and go on to give plausible-sounding reasons for choices they did not make.

At the end of each of these studies, the experimenters reveal the original survey and reversed responses, and the subjects are typically surprised and bemused at their own behavior. The beliefs they had taken to be strongly held turned out to be props that they could pick up and set aside as needed. These studies do not demonstrate that people lack political convictions, but they do show that, in at least some cases, the reasons we articulate to explain our decisions are not the real basis of those decisions. Such experiments cast doubt on whether our political principles really form the bedrock for our opinions as we assume. Our principles are, at best, just one source of information that shapes our political beliefs at any moment.

Daily life, of course, rarely involves sneaky psychologists plotting to upend our opinions. Simply directing people's attention to different aspects of their own lives can have a similar effect. In one study psychologist Christopher Bryan and colleagues surveyed undergraduate students at Stanford about their political opinions, including such topics as universal health care coverage, a flat tax, welfare and unemployment benefits, the death penalty, and other issues on which liberals and conservatives disagree. Before they completed the survey, however, the students were asked to spend ten minutes telling the story of how they got into Stanford. Half were asked specifically to comment on the role of their own "hard work, self-discipline and wise decisions," while the other were asked to comment on the role of "chance, opportunity and help from others." Gaining admission to an elite university like Stanford requires both individual merit and good fortune, so both groups had plenty to write about.

This seemingly minor shift in attention led to substantial differences in political attitudes on the survey. The group asked to consider their personal merit expressed more conservative opinions than the group that contemplated its good fortune. Regardless of their ideologies when they walked in the door, simply thinking about the role of individual merit or opportunities in their own lives affected their political viewpoints, at least for a while.

Emotion can be even more powerful than thoughts. Recall when you first heard about the planes that flew into the World Trade Center on September 11, 2001. Most Americans (and many non-Americans, too) remember exactly where they were and what they were doing at that moment. For me, it was an old friend calling from Manhattan to say he was fine. I woke befuddled in an earlier time zone, turning on CNN to watch as the second plane struck. In my memory, the fog of waking is fused with the confusion of the event. My mental images of the smoldering white towers against a bright blue sky are punctuated by my questioning whether I was dreaming something that could not possibly be happening.

In the days that followed the terrorist attack, George W. Bush's approval rating rose from 51 percent to 90 percent, the highest recorded presidential approval rating in history. Millions of Americans who were antagonistic to the president on September 10 reversed their opinions almost overnight. The 9/11 attacks were not the first external threat America endured. Similar, though less pronounced, "rally 'round the flag effects" have been documented for other events, like the bombing of Pearl Harbor or the Iran hostage crisis. History shows, however, that conservative administrations have benefited more from this kind of rallying than liberal administrations. If Jost is right that people adopt conservative ideologies as a response against threats to the social order, then there should be a specific link between threats and support for conservative ideas.

In fact, there are decades' worth of studies supporting that association. Many of them examine correlations between people's personalities and their political beliefs. In study after study, subjects who see the world as a threatening and dangerous place tend to be more politically conservative. Those who see the world as safe, and who are motivated by exploring and trying new experiences, tend to support more liberal views. Of course, these correlations leave open the question of cause and effect. Do these emotional tendencies predispose people toward particular political ideologies, as the theory predicts? Or do conservative versus liberal mind-sets lead people to tune in to different emotional channels? Or are they both just a reflection of some other factor that causes both?

Several experiments have begun to isolate the specific relationship between emotions and ideologies. In one study, psychologists Alan Lambert, Laura Scherer, and colleagues made people feel threatened by showing them a video documentary about the 9/11 attacks. Compared with a control group that simply completed some word puzzles, the 9/11 group expressed greater support for President Bush, more hawkish attitudes about the war in Iraq, and more liking for patriotic symbols like the American flag and the Statue of Liberty. Psychologist Mark Landau and colleagues asked a group of research subjects to vividly imagine what it would be like to die. They instructed them to describe their feelings in detail and to envision what would happen to their body after death. Compared with a control group, the death group was more supportive of President Bush and less supportive of John Kerry, who was running against him in the 2004 election at the time of the study.

Field studies lead to the same conclusion as the laboratory studies. The years following the 9/11 attacks were anxious ones for Americans. The newly formed Department of Homeland Security introduced a Terror Advisory System complete with a color-coded guide to alert citizens whether the risk of a terror attack was low (green), elevated (yellow), high (orange), or severe (red). Sociologist Robb Willer analyzed presidential approval ratings between 2001 and 2004 and found that whenever the terror alert increased, so, too, did approval ratings for President Bush. When the alerts subsided, presidential approval fell with them. The ebb and flow of threats from one day to the next pulls our ideologies in tow.

We normally speak of conservatives and liberals, not conservative moments and liberal moments. The truth is that we experience both. Sometimes we think through an issue based on our principles and end up at an ideological conclusion. At other times we take our cues from a particular situation and find an ideology that fits the moment. When we reflect on our own beliefs, it can be nearly impossible to tell the difference between the two approaches.

Of all the cues that nudge us to the left or the right, the role of wealth, poverty, and inequality has been one of the most vexing topics in recent memory. Our culture has conflicting narratives about how the haves and have-nots differ in their politics. Consider the lives of two very different individuals.

Earl drives a truck for a living, and mostly makes daylong trips like the ones to haul front loaders and excavators from Murfreesboro to Fort Wayne. When he gets home in the evening, he likes to open a can of beer and watch the local news. On the weekends, he views NASCAR races. When he misses one, he checks up on the driver standings in the newspaper, and still has the paper version delivered. Apart from that, he doesn't have a lot of hobbies. When his youngest child left home, he thought he would take up gardening, but his weekends are more and more occupied with working on his aging house trailer. He's got far more money in the Kenworth rig parked outside than in his home. He has rarely used the sleeper cabin in the truck, but it's always an option if the house's roof gets too bad.

David is on his third landscaper this year. The first was unreliable; the second kept chopping off the heads of the lawn sprinklers with the mower. Now his lawn is finally getting in shape to suit his newly built home on the cul-de-sac. He likes to say he designed it himself, but what he means is that he and his wife, Andrea, picked the finishes from the laminated pages of the builder's book. They saved for the house for five years and wanted it to be perfect, with four bedrooms plus an office, because they work a lot at home in the evenings. There's also an extra room that they use for fitness, so that their free weights and yoga mats are always at the ready. But they are proudest of the screened porch, where they drink coffee in the mornings from David's newest gadget, which siphons water through a series of glass tubes like a nineteenth-century science kit. As they sip, David reads the news on his phone and Andrea listens to NPR. Lately they've been discussing investing more for retirement.

It's amazing how much we can tell about people from these little glimpses into their lives. After such a brief introduction, do you feel that you know other things about Earl and David? Such as, who's more likely to go out for sushi? Who communicates with family members by yelling across the house, and who walks into the next room and speaks quietly? Who spent months agonizing over which school to send their children to?

Would you be surprised to learn that Earl is a born-again Christian and that he opposes same-sex marriage, but David thinks that gay people should be able to wed? You might also not be surprised to discover that David supports laws to restrict handgun ownership, but Earl supports the NRA. Or that Earl prefers a "small government" and thinks that income taxes should be cut.

You know the answers, of course. They are supplied by the images of conservatives and liberals rendered in fine detail in our heads. We can envision the conservatives packing the family off to church in the pickup truck to the tune of country music. We can imagine the liberals returning from the farmers' market, careful not to blemish their heirloom tomatoes as they drive home in the Prius, listening to a podcast of David Sedaris. You can even distinguish their ideologies in their consumption patterns. Liberals drive Land Rovers and Lexuses, while conservatives prefer Pontiacs and Buicks. Liberals drink Sam Adams Light, while conservatives drink Bud. Liberals eat kale salads at Panera, while conservatives eat chicken-fried steaks at Cracker Barrel.

This division between liberal elites and working-class conservatives seems to be reflected in voting patterns as well. For example, who do you think is more likely to have voted for Barack Obama—Earl or David? This division between liberal elites and working-class conservatives poses a big puzzle. As many writers have argued, people seem to vote against their own self-interests. Less well-off conservatives vote for leaders who pass tax cuts that mainly benefit the wealthy while cutting government benefits that help the poor. One explanation for this paradox, as recounted in Thomas Frank's bestselling book *What's the Matter with Kansas?*, is that a small number of wealthy elites in the Republican Party have duped working-class Americans into voting for policies that favor the rich by riling them up with concerns about "God, guns, and gays." These cultural issues arouse so much anger, the theory goes, that people will vote for economic policies that do not benefit them.

The satirical news site *The Onion* perfectly summed up this sentiment following George W. Bush's reelection in an article headlined "Nation's Poor Win Election for Nation's Rich":

> "The Republican party—the party of industrial mega-capitalists, corporate financiers, power brokers, and the moneyed elite—would like to thank the undereducated rural poor, the struggling blue-collar workers in Middle America, and the God-fearing underprivileged minorities who voted George W. Bush back into office," Karl Rove, senior advisor to Bush, told reporters at a press conference Monday. "You have selflessly sacrificed your well-being and voted against your own economic interest. For this, we humbly thank you." Added Rove: "You have acted beyond the call of duty—or, for that matter, good sense."

The trouble is that this whole account is wrong. It's not only wrong, but it's almost perfectly backward.

It is simply not true that most poor people vote conservative and most rich people vote liberal. Far from it. The fact is that the higher a person's income is, the more likely he is to vote Republican. The richest third of the population votes more Republican than the middle third, who vote more Republican than the bottom third.

Political scientist Andrew Gelman has documented these trends using data from the American National Elections Studies and the National Annenberg Election Survey, as well as from state and national exit polls. These surveys are carried out using

Figure 4.2. Electoral map of the 2004 presidential election. Dark states indicate Republican wins, light states indicate Democrat wins. Adapted from Gelman (2006).

painstaking methods to guarantee that they are representative of the American population, and they all tell the same story. Although no income group is monolithic, the trend is clear: The richer you are, the more likely you are to call yourself a Republican and to vote Republican. The poorer you are, the more likely you are to call yourself a Democrat and to vote Democrat.

Consider the electoral map, shown in Figure 4.2, for the 2004 presidential election. Dark states voted for George W. Bush and light states voted for John Kerry. This is one source of our mistaken images of rich and poor voters. We look at affluent coastal states like New York and California and see a population of latte-sipping liberals. We look at the poor red states in the middle of the country and picture them as the home of poor, God-fearing conservatives. But as Gelman points out, these state-level summaries ignore the incomes of the individuals within those states. If we break down the vote tallies by the incomes of the voters, we see an entirely different picture.

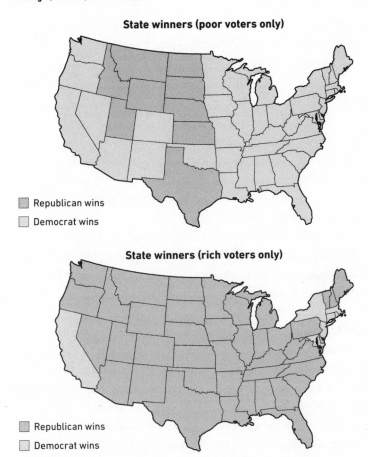

Figure 4.3. What the electoral map of the 2004 presidential election would look like if we counted only the votes of the poor (top) and rich (bottom). Dark states indicate Republican wins, light states indicate Democrat wins. Adapted from Gelman (2006).

The maps in Figure 4.3 show the same electoral map of the 2004 election, redrawn based on the incomes of the voters. The top image shows what the electoral map would look like if we counted only the votes of poor people—a landslide victory for Democrats. The second image shows what the electoral map would look like if we counted only the votes of the rich—a landslide win for the

Republicans. Money matters, and in the opposite direction from our stereotypical images of red and blue Americans.

What of the differences in tastes and styles between liberals and conservatives? Political campaign advertisers have spent a lot of time collecting data on the consumer preferences of voters in each party. It turns out that Land Rovers and Lexuses are two of the most Republican cars there are. Land Rover owners, for example, favor the Republican Party over the Democratic Party by about 30 percentage points. Pontiac and Buick owners, in contrast, skew Democratic. You may be surprised to learn that Chevy, Ford, and Volvo are all evenly split.

The stereotypical images of partisan dining habits have been shown to be mistaken, too. Both Cracker Barrel and Panera attract more Republicans than Democrats. Democrats apparently prefer Golden Corral and Dunkin' Donuts (who knew?). We even get the beers wrong. Contrary to popular belief, Republicans love Sam Adams Light and Democrats drink most of the Budweiser. Our latte-sipping, farmers' market–shopping liberals might be horrified to learn that the most Democratic beer of all is Milwaukee's Best. The most Republican beer of all isn't even made in America: It's the Dutch import Amstel Light.

Typecasting consumption patterns based on political affiliation isn't always wrong. Democrats really do buy most of the Priuses, and Republicans really do watch more Fox News. But these expressions of taste are directly related to the political ideologies that matter to members of each party. People choose hybrids because they are concerned about climate change. People tune in to Fox News because it presents the right-wing perspectives they want to hear. As we drift further away from actual political issues, however, our images of liberals and conservatives become flimsier and turn into empty stereotypes that are more likely to mislead us.

As strange as this all sounds to those of us accustomed to standard conceptions of liberal elites and salt-of-the-earth conservatives, the patterns outlined by Gelman make perfect sense to economists and political scientists. Every capitalist economy in the world has some degree of free market competition, as well as some degree of market regulation and taxation. Both exist on a continuum, and no serious thinker on the left or right believes you can entirely eliminate either one. Tax rates close to 100 percent completely stifle motivation and innovation. The collapse of communist systems in the twentieth century is generally seen as evidence that extreme levels of government regulation and taxation cannot compete with free market economies. At the other extreme, an entirely unregulated market would quickly lead to monopolies, which would defeat the purpose of market competition. Lack of taxation would lead to the deterioration of roads and other infrastructure, as well as military defense.

In the real world, market economies exist in a middle ground between these extremes. Every capitalist country has some form of regulation, some form of taxation, and some form of safety net for those at the bottom. Economic debates between liberals and conservatives are ultimately about pushing the needle a little more in one direction or the other. Conservative policies aim to promote the free market, while liberal ones seek greater taxation to support shared infrastructure and safety net programs.

Economists have argued for decades that rational political choices (rational in the sense of narrowly defined self-interest) depend on how much money you have. When it comes to issues like shared infrastructure, such as roads and military defense, everyone benefits about the same. But safety net programs help the poor more than the rich, so the more money you earn, the more sense it makes to support lower taxes and less redistribution of wealth. The less money you earn, the more incentive you have to support higher taxation and redistribution. In this framework, people seem to conform to economists' image of rational, calculating agents making decisions based on their economic self-interest.

They appear to fit that model, that is, until you assess people's understanding of what is in their self-interest. In one study, researchers surveyed people who were recipients of a variety of government-subsidized benefits. They asked the subjects a simple question: Have you ever used a government social program? Remarkably, nearly half believed that they had not. Forty percent of those receiving Medicare, for example, denied ever obtaining government benefits. The same was claimed by 47 percent of those receiving the Earned Income Tax Credit. More than half of people receiving government-subsidized student loans said they had not taken any government benefits. These subjects weren't lying. Medicare recipients, for example, would acknowledge that they had received Medicare, but they just didn't believe that it had anything to do with the government. Surveys like this suggest that people have almost no idea whether government programs are in their economic self-interest.

Maybe people don't understand the extent of government benefits, but are they aware of whether raising or lowering taxes benefits them? Political scientist Larry Bartels asked how well people know what is in their self-interest when it comes to tax cuts. His answer is best summed up in the title of the article he wrote about his results: "Homer Gets a Tax Cut." Bartels studied the opinions of Americans regarding the tax cuts passed during the George W. Bush administration. These measures had major consequences, amounting to trillions of dollars. Still, when asked whether they favored the cuts, opposed them, or hadn't thought about the issue, 40 percent of respondents said they hadn't thought about it. When asked factual questions about the cuts and their consequences, most people either didn't know the answers or got them wrong.

Not everybody is a political news junkie, of course, so Bartels tried to determine whether people might have more knowledge about tax cuts if they were more knowledgeable about politics in general. The survey included a seven-question quiz to measure how conversant with the topic the respondents were. The questions were not especially difficult. One, for example, asked what position Dick Cheney held (he was vice president at the time); another asked who Tony Blair was. While knowledge about tax cuts was higher among people who were well informed about politics, unfortunately very few people were in that category. Most subjects got more questions wrong than right. If the questionnaire had been a classroom test, most Americans would have flunked.

How, then, does the average American manage to vote in ways that benefit him economically? One clue comes from the power of feeling poor, as we saw in Chapter 1. That feeling depends not just on one's own wealth but also on how it compares to that of other people, as we saw in Chapter 2. Gelman's research on voting and income provides one clue about the importance of relative comparisons. The tendency for the rich to vote Republican is stronger in poor states than in rich ones. So, if you are a wealthy Mississippian, you are much more likely to vote Republican than if you have the same wealth in New York or Connecticut. Although the reason is not completely understood, I suspect it has to do with the different kinds of relative comparisons people make in rich and poor states. If you earn $200,000 a year in Biloxi, then you likely feel much richer than most people around you. But if you make the same income in Manhattan, you may feel barely middle class.

My colleagues and I suspected that those social comparisons might affect the way people think about political issues more than their actual wealth does. We focused on the kinds of policies that economists argue are most clearly linked to economic self-interest: taxation and redistribution of wealth. To test that idea, we set out to change people's social comparisons to see whether changes in political opinions followed. We asked a group of participants to answer a long computerized survey about their incomes, spending habits, shopping tastes, and even personality traits. We then provided them with computerized feedback. Although the participants thought that the feedback was based on their survey answers, in reality we randomly assigned them to receive one of two kinds of response. The first group was told that they had more money than most other people who were similar to them in their demographics and personality. The other group was told that they had less money than most others who were comparable to them. We then asked both groups a series of questions about their views on political issues, including taxation and redistribution.

As we predicted, participants who felt relatively rich expressed less support for redistribution, while those who were made to feel relatively poor became more supportive. These two groups had the same average income and the same average level of education. All that differed was whether they felt richer or poorer than their peers. Social comparisons led to differences in political beliefs.

This study also suggests that citizens in general do vote in their economic interest despite being mostly ill informed about where that interest really lies. Imagine that people who *feel* better off than average vote to cut taxes and to cut welfare benefits, and those who *feel* poorer than average vote to raise taxes and increase welfare benefits. Since feelings of relative status are (modestly) linked to actual incomes, people will be right about their self-interest more often than they are wrong. The result is that voting patterns that seem random at the individual level approximate patterns of self-interested voting, on average. Like a murmuration of starlings, millions of people looking myopically at where they stand compared with their neighbors can produce a group that seems to move with purpose.

We've seen so far that people tend to vote for policies that they feel are in their self-interest whether they actually are or not. And we've seen that what feels to be in their self-interest depends on how they compare with other people. As the haves and the have-nots grow further apart, we can expect the effects of social comparisons to weigh more and more heavily. Taken together, these observations suggest that the rise in inequality that has occurred over the past few decades might be contributing to increasingly intense partisanship and political conflict.

It is hard to escape the conclusion that politics in America has become more polarized in recent years. The data support that observation. Geoscientist Clio Andris and her colleagues used data analysis techniques developed for mapping geographical distances to map the "distances" between members of different parties in the U.S. House of Representatives based on roll call votes. Whenever two representatives vote the same way, they are drawn closer to each other. When they vote differently, they become further apart. The results are striking.

Figure 4.4 shows the distances between each representative for the Congresses of 1981, 1991, 2001, and 2011. Each House member is represented by a single black dot (Republicans) or gray dot (Democrats). In the 1980s there was a lot of overlap. Many of the gray dots are deep into black territory, and many of the black dots are in gray territory. The border between the two is thin and permeable. With

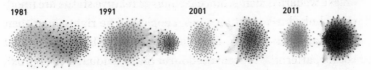

Figure 4.4. Graphical depiction of polarization over time in the U.S. Congress. Adapted from Adris et al., 2015.

each decade, however, the overlap recedes. By 2011 both sides were almost perfectly sealed off from each other, and the middle ground is a no-man's-land. These visualizations vividly illustrate the polarization that has split political elites over the past four decades. Does inequality contribute to this division?

To answer that question, we went back to the laboratory. We ran an experiment in which participants were presented with several stocks. The subjects read about each company that issued the stock, its price-to-earnings ratio, and how the stock had performed over the last six months. They then chose how to invest some seed money, provided by the experimenters, in whatever combination of stocks they wanted. They were told that the performance of the securities would be simulated based on real stock market performance from the previous six months, and that they could keep whatever profit they earned from the investments. In reality, everyone made a 30 percent profit on their investments, but half of the participants were told that they did better than 89 percent of other players, while the other half were told that they did worse than 89 percent. In this way, we created differences in relative status, without there being any differences in actual money earned.

A crucial part of this experiment was that it evolved. The current rules, we told participants, had been created by the votes of past players. One rule was that high earners would be taxed 20 percent of their earnings to offset the losses endured by low earners, who would be given a 20 percent bonus. In other words, the game included a redistribution policy. To find out whether relative status would change opinions about redistribution, we then asked the participants to vote on how the rules should change for future generations of players. As we expected based on the role of relative status, the higher-status group wanted to cut taxes and reduce redistribution, and the lower-status group wanted to increase taxes and benefits for future generations of players.

We then presented our subjects with the recommendations of

another player who either agreed with them or disagreed with them about the redistribution issue, and asked what they thought of that player. Was the other player competent or incompetent? Was he guided by principle or biased by self-interest? Was he even paying attention to the rules of the game? Was he a rational decision maker or an irrational fool?

As expected, subjects judged the other player to be more incompetent, more biased, and less rational when he disagreed with the subject than when he agreed. When we looked closer at the data, though, we noticed an interesting detail: The perception of the other player as biased and irrational was driven entirely by the group who were told that they did better than their peers. Something about feeling superior in profits made people feel superior to other players about their opinions, too.

We have a tendency to think that people who agree with us are brilliant and insightful, and that those who disagree with us could use a little help in seeing reality for what it is. As George Carlin put it, "Have you ever noticed that anybody driving slower than you is an idiot, and anyone going faster than you is a maniac?" This propensity to believe that we see the world accurately, while anyone who has a different opinion is benighted, fuels conflicts. As psychologist Lee Ross has argued, if I see the world as it is and you disagree with me, then I have only a few possible interpretations of your behavior: You might be incompetent, you might be irrational, or you might be evil. Whatever the case, I can't reason with you.

If these differences in perception are especially powerful among people who feel rich, then we face some worrying implications as inequality continues to increase. As the minority at the top pull further and further away from the mass of working-class people at the bottom, we can expect their political opinions to change. They will mistake their self-interests for genuine principles, and they will look with disdain on people who disagree with them. If they view their political opponents as incompetent, irrational, or immoral, then they won't be motivated to compromise.

To determine whether feeling rich really has the potential to influence these beliefs, we ran a final experiment using the investment game. As before, everyone picked stocks, everyone made the same profit, and one group thought they did better than others while the other group thought they did worse. They were again presented with the redistribution recommendations of another player who either agreed or disagreed with them. This time, though, in addition to asking what subjects thought of the other player, we told them that the other player would take part in voting on the rules for the next generation of players, and that his vote would count as much as everyone else's. One of the rules that they could change, however, was whether every vote should be counted equally.

The results were sobering. The subjects who thought their earnings were inferior wanted to increase redistribution, as before. But they wanted everyone's vote to count equally, regardless of whether the other player agreed or disagreed with them. The subjects who thought they were superior wanted to reduce redistribution, and they also voted to reject the votes of those who disagreed with them. The more they saw the other player as incompetent and irrational, the less they wanted his vote to count. This research was the first to show that feeling superior in status magnifies our feeling that we see reality as it is while our opponents are deluded. It supports the idea that as the top and the bottom of the social ladder drift further apart, our politics will become more divisive. That is exactly what has happened over the past several decades.

Political scientist Nolan McCarty and his colleagues have also traced political divisions over the last century in the U.S. House of Representatives and Senate, formulating a measure of polarization based on how lawmakers vote, similar to the data used for Andris's graphs. The polarization index is at its highest when all Democrats vote one way and all Republicans vote the other. Using this index,

Income Inequality and Political Polarization
1947–2012

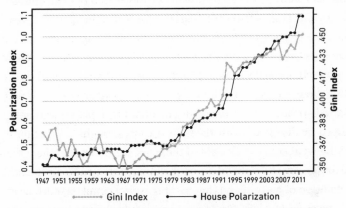

Figure 4.5. The Gini index of inequality and political polarization in the House of Representatives rose in lockstep since the 1970s. From McCarty, Poole, & Rosenthal (2016).

they calculated how polarized American politics has been in every Congress since 1947. Figure 4.5 shows that polarization in the House of Representatives and the Gini index of inequality have followed strikingly similar trajectories. Results for the Senate are similar. Both inequality and polarization were relatively low through the 1950s and 1960s. They then began rising in tandem in the mid-1970s and have remained on par ever since.

Behavioral experiments and historical data both point to the same conclusion: As our economic worlds diverge, so, too, do our politics. It becomes ever more difficult to see those on the other side of the aisle as well-meaning individuals who share our goals but differ in what they believe are the best means to reach them. Instead, the other side begins to look more and more like enemies.

Leslie Rutledge is the attorney general of Arkansas. When she was elected in 2014, she had to work harder than expected for one vote—her own. Rutledge is a Republican who supported Arkansas's 2013 voter ID law, which requires voters to show a government-issued ID at polling places. Democrats objected that the law was a thinly disguised effort to prevent poor people and minorities from voting because they are less likely to have valid IDs. Republicans argued that strict standards at the ballot box were important to prevent fraud. Arkansas law also requires citizens to be registered in the state and nowhere else in order to vote. So when the Democratic county clerk, Larry Crane, saw that Rutledge was still registered in Washington, D.C., where she had previously lived, he canceled her voter registration.

Rutledge accused Crane of using "Chicago-style politics" to "disenfranchise" her. Arkansas Democrats enjoyed a few days of schadenfreude and wrote many blog posts about the true meaning of irony.

What do you think were the Arkansas Republicans' true motives in passing the voter ID law? What do you think Crane's real motives were in dropping Rutledge from the voter rolls? Regardless of who you believe was right or wrong in this case, you are likely to be confident that you are assessing the situation with clear eyes, and that anyone who disagrees with you is willfully ignorant at best and malevolent at worst. Polls from the Pew Research Center have revealed that the percentage of ordinary Americans who have a "very unfavorable" opinion of the opposing political party has steadily grown over the last three decades as inequality has increased. In 2014, about a third of respondents thought that members of the opposite party were not just mistaken, but were a threat to the nation's well-being. A third of conservatives and a quarter of liberals said that they would be upset if a family member married someone of the wrong party. These trends are dangerous, because when opponents become enemies, people can justify almost anything in responding to them. After all, how can you expect to reason with idiots and maniacs?

Chapter 5

Long Lives and Tall Tombstones

Inequality Is a Matter of Life and Death

t's late October, and I am kneeling in Old Chapel Hill Cemetery, brushing the fallen leaves from a small, flat stone sunken into the earth. *Percy R. Baker, June 23, 1913–May 11, 1966.* A few more weeks and he would have turned fifty-three. Several feet away I am startled by a marker the size of a lunch box that is half covered by a shrub. *Thomas W. Battle, Jr., Mar. 15, 1918–May 10, 1918.*

On the other side of the cemetery stands an imposing stone monument the size of an upright piano. In letters large enough to read from yards away, it reads: *William F. Strowd, 1832–1911.* The memorial documents that he was a devout man, a member of the North Carolina Constitutional Convention, and a member of the United States Congress. Strowd lived to the age of seventy-nine, impressive in an era when the life expectancy was fifty-one. Nearby is an extravagant obelisk taller than a man, bearing a coat of arms in gold against black granite, marking the grave sites of Eugene Simpson, who lived seventy-nine years, and Margaret Simpson, who lived to eighty-five.

I did not know the descendants of the Bakers or the Battles or the Simpsons, but I had just read about a research finding so curious that I had to test it for myself. You could predict the life span recorded on a tombstone, the study claimed, by the size of the monument. The explanation for this, of course, is money: The

Life Expectancy at Birth vs. Average Annual Income

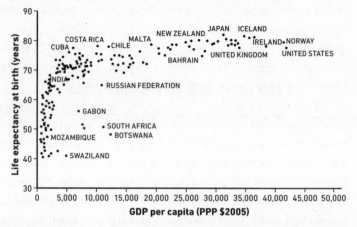

Figure 5.1. Effects of per capita income on life expectancy level off after countries reach a basic level of development.

wealthier you are, the longer you live, and the bigger the tombstone your family can afford. This link between longevity and tombstone size was documented by George Davey Smith, an epidemiologist in Scotland. His team roamed the graveyards of Glasgow, recording the height of the gravestones and the birth and death dates inscribed on them. He found that each meter of height was associated with a little more than two additional years of life. I brought my class of undergraduates out to the campus graveyard equipped with tape measures to test whether we would find the same relationship at another time and place. Sure enough, we found the same phenomenon in Chapel Hill: Longer lives were recorded on larger stones.

There are a lot of reasons, of course, why poverty could be bad for one's health. The poor may do without basic medical care, safe living conditions, and good sanitation. If conditions are truly desperate, they might die of hunger. More commonly, malnourished children fail to develop healthy immune systems and can die from common infections, like measles. Those two sources of death to-gether make up the statistics we occasionally hear that a child dies of hunger every eight seconds (or ten seconds, or fifteen; as global poverty has been reduced over the last decade, that grim statistic is dropping). You can see the difference in life expectancy between rich and poor countries in Figure 5.1.

When we examine the data within individual countries, we also see a very clear link between money and health. The more money you have, the better your health and the longer you are likely to live. Take, for example, the difference in death rates across the richest and poorest zip codes in America. In the richest zip codes, the annual death rate is about 50 deaths per 10,000 people. In the poorest zip codes, that number nearly doubles to 90 deaths per 10,000. Each step up in wealth translates into extra years in life.

We can see this pattern even more clearly in data from a massive study of more than ten thousand British Civil Service employees

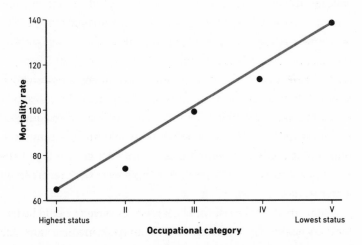

Figure 5.2. Social status and mortality rates are linearly related within rich countries. This example is from Marmot's study of British civil servants (2004).

that has been in progress since the 1960s. Her Majesty's Civil Service has an exquisitely detailed hierarchy, with dozens of clearly defined job grades from cabinet secretaries who report directly to the prime minister all the way down to entry-level clerical jobs. Physician Michael Marmot has found that each rung down the ladder is associated with a shorter life span. The pattern is strikingly linear, so that even the difference between the highest-status government officials and those just one rung below was linked to increased mortality (see Figure 5.2).

The Scottish gravestone research also included a telling detail that sheds further light on the nature of the link between money and health. Smith notes that the graves they studied belonged mostly to middle- and upper-class people. (The poor were often buried with no gravestone, or with a wooden marker that did not survive the elements.) That particular fact may not sound very significant, but it offers a clue to a much bigger truth about how wealth shapes health.

In the story "Silver Blaze," Sherlock Holmes investigates the murder of a horse trainer and the disappearance of his famous racehorse the night before a contest. A Scotland Yard detective asks Holmes, "Is there any other point to which you would wish to draw my attention?" Holmes answers, "To the curious incident of the dog in the night-time." "The dog did nothing in the night-time," says the detective. To which Holmes replies, "That was the curious incident." The dog that didn't bark tells Holmes that the horse thief must have been an insider, familiar to the dog. It takes Holmes's extraordinary wit to notice the absence of evidence as evidence. For their part, it took scientists a while to realize that there was something missing from the graph relating money to life span within developed countries.

If you look carefully at Figure 5.1, you'll notice that the curve comparing different countries is bent. The relatively small income advantage that India has over Mozambique, for example, translates into much longer lives in India. Once countries reach the level of development of Chile or Costa Rica, something interesting happens: The curve flattens out. Very rich countries like the United States cease to have any life expectancy advantage over moderately rich countries like Bahrain or even Cuba. At a certain level of economic development, increases in average income stop mattering much.

But within a rich country, there is no bend; the relationship between money and longevity remains linear. If the relationship was driven by high mortality rates among the very poor, you would expect to see a bend. That is, you would expect dramatically shorter lives among the very poor, and then, once above the poverty line, additional income would have little effect. This curious absence of the bend in the line suggests that the link between money and health is not actually a reflection of poverty per se, at least not among economically developed countries. If it was extreme poverty driving the effect, then there would be a big spike in mortality among the very poorest and little difference between the middle- and highest-status groups.

The linear pattern in the British Civil Service study is also striking, because the subjects in this study all have decent government jobs and the salaries, health insurance, pensions, and other benefits that are associated with them. If you thought that elevated mortality rates were only a function of the desperately poor being unable to meet their basic needs, this study would disprove that, because it did not include any desperately poor subjects and still found elevated mortality among those with lower status.

Psychologist Nancy Adler and colleagues have found that where people place themselves on the Status Ladder is a better predictor of health than their actual income or education. In fact, in collaboration with Marmot, Adler's team revisited the study of British civil servants and asked the research subjects to rate themselves on the

Life Expectancy (United Nations report 2004)

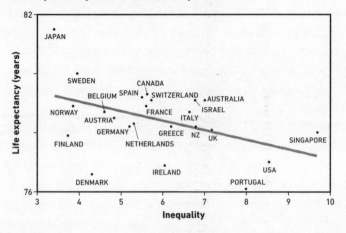

Figure 5.3. Among economically developed countries, higher inequality is associated with shorter life expectancies.

ladder. Their subjective assessments of where they stood compared with others proved to be a better predictor of their health than their occupational status. Adler's analyses suggest that occupational status shapes subjective status, and this subjective feeling of one's standing, in turn, affects health.

If health and longevity in developed countries are more closely linked to relative comparisons than to income, then you would expect that societies with greater inequality would have poorer health. And, in fact, they do. Across the developed nations surveyed by Wilkinson and Pickett, those with greater income equality had longer life expectancies (see Figure 5.3). Likewise, in the United States, people who lived in states with greater income equality lived longer (see Figure 5.4). Both of these relationships remain once we statistically control for average income, which means that inequality in incomes, not just income itself, is responsible.

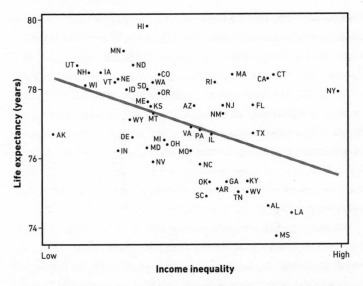

Figure 5.4. In the U.S., states with higher inequality tend to have shorter life expectancies.

But how can something as abstract as inequality or social comparisons cause something as physical as health? Our emergency rooms are not filled with people dropping dead from acute cases of inequality. No, the pathways linking inequality to health can be traced through specific maladies, especially heart disease, cancer, diabetes, and health problems stemming from obesity. Abstract ideas that start as macroeconomic policies and social relationships somehow get expressed in the functioning of our cells.

To understand how that expression happens, we have to first realize that people from different walks of life die different kinds of deaths, in part because they live different kinds of lives. We saw in Chapter 2 that people in more unequal states and countries have poor outcomes on many health measures, including violence, infant mortality, obesity and diabetes, mental illness, and more. In Chapter 3 we learned that inequality leads people to take greater risks, and uncertain futures lead people to take an impulsive, live fast, die young approach to life. There are clear connections between the temptation to enjoy immediate pleasures versus denying oneself for the benefit of long-term health. We saw, for example, that inequality was linked to risky behaviors. In places with extreme inequality, people are more likely to abuse drugs and alcohol, more likely to have unsafe sex, and so on. Other research suggests that living in a high-inequality state increases people's likelihood of smoking, eating too much, and exercising too little.

Taken together, this evidence implies that inequality leads to illness and shorter lives in part because it gives rise to unhealthy behaviors. That conclusion has been very controversial, especially on the political left. Some argue that it blames the victim because it implies that the poor and those who live in high-inequality areas are partly responsible for their fates by making bad choices. But I don't think it's assigning blame to point out the obvious fact that health is affected by smoking, drinking too much, poor diet and exercise, and so on. It becomes a matter of blaming the victim only if you assume that these behaviors are exclusively the result of the weak characters of the less fortunate. On the contrary, we have seen plenty of evidence that poverty and inequality have effects on the thinking and decision making of people living in those conditions. If you or I were thrust into such situations, we might well start behaving in more unhealthy ways, too.

The link between inequality and unhealthy behaviors helps shed light on a surprising trend discovered in a 2015 paper by economists Anne Case and Angus Deaton. Death rates have been steadily declining in the United States and throughout the economically developed world for decades, but these authors noticed a glaring exception: Since the 1990s, the death rate for middle-aged white

Americans has been rising. The increase is concentrated among men and whites without a college degree. The death rate for black Americans of the same age remains higher, but is trending slowly downward, like that of all other minority groups.

The wounds in this group seem to be largely self-inflicted. They are not dying from higher rates of heart disease or cancer. They are dying of cirrhosis of the liver, suicide, and a cycle of chronic pain and overdoses of opiates and painkillers.

The trend itself is striking because it speaks to the power of subjective social comparisons. This demographic group is dying of violated expectations. Although high school–educated whites make more money on average than similarly educated blacks, the whites expect more because of their history of privilege. Widening income inequality and stagnant social mobility, Case and Deaton suggest, mean that this generation is likely to be the first in American history that is not more affluent than its parents.

Unhealthy behaviors among those who feel left behind can explain part of the link between inequality and health, but only part. The best estimates have found that such behavior accounts for about one third of the association between inequality and health. Much of the rest is a function of how the body itself responds to crises. Just as our decisions and actions prioritize short-term gains over longer-term interests when in a crisis, the body has a sophisticated mechanism that adopts the same strategy. This crisis management system is specifically designed to save you now, even if it has to shorten your life to do so.

The system is called the stress response. Stress is the body's original payday loan. For such a remarkable system, stress was discovered rather late, operating in plain sight for eons before anyone realized the effect it was having. János Hugo Bruno "Hans" Selye was a young Hungarian endocrinologist at McGill University in the 1930s. His research at the time involved injecting rats with chemicals extracted from rat ovaries to measure their effects on the animals' bodies, and ideally to identify a new hormone.

At first the experiment looked like a huge success. The rats treated with the ovarian extract showed enlargements of certain glands, while other glands shrank, and the subjects developed stomach ulcers. Something was happening, and it looked very much like a new hormonal effect. Selye then examined his control group of rats, which had been injected with a different kind of hormonal extract. The puzzling thing was that they showed the same symptoms. So he tried another kind of extract, and then another. In trial after trial, whatever he injected into the rats seemed to have the same physical results.

Rather than discovering the unique effects of some unknown hormone, Selye had stumbled on a response to . . . what exactly? Having material injected into one's body? Being poked with needles? Selye did more studies to determine precisely what kinds of traumas it took to generate the symptoms. The studies involved the kind of grim procedures that would probably never be allowed by research ethics boards today. He injected other chemicals, like morphine and formaldehyde. He cut some rats' skin and broke the bones of others. He placed some in freezing cold, and others were starved for days.

Following each experiment, Selye dissected the rats and carefully noted the bodily consequences of each particular type of treatment. He ultimately discovered that the rats showed virtually the same pattern of biological responses to every kind of distress.

His results reminded him of something that he had noticed years earlier as a medical student. His professor had presented students with five patients to observe, each suffering from a different ailment. The point of the exercise was to get the students to notice the unique symptoms that marked each disease, like the little red spots that differentiated the measles from the flu. But what Selye had found most striking was that all of the patients shared many symptoms, like fever, loss of appetite, aches and pains, and swollen tonsils. When Selye suggested that there seemed to be a "syndrome of just being sick," his professor was not impressed, and his idea went nowhere. Until, that is, Selye noticed the same generality in rats' symptoms regardless of the treatments to which they were exposed.

Selye first called this "general adaptation syndrome" and later renamed it simply "stress." The idea was unpopular among physiologists, who were primarily interested in mapping the links between particular chemicals and particular bodily effects. They thought of the body as something like a Swiss army knife, with a special tool for every job, or a collection of delicate keys to open each intricate lock. But Selye was saying that things were much messier than that. Disturb the system in any way, and you get this same generalized response. His supervising professor called it the "pharmacology of dirt."

Selye had many of the details wrong. He thought, for example, that long-term stress was harmful because the body ran out of stress hormones and couldn't replenish them quickly enough, leaving the body unguarded once the hormones ran out. And his motivations were called into question when evidence later emerged that he had been funded heavily by tobacco companies, which used his research to argue that it wasn't cigarettes, but stress, that was dangerous: People simply smoked to relieve stress.

The concept of stress as a general bodily reaction to any kind of crisis has, however, withstood the test of time. Today we understand the stress response as the way the body prepares to expend a great deal of energy to respond to a threat or an opportunity.

To understand how stress works, imagine that you are a hunter-gatherer type searching for food on the grasslands. Suddenly, you hear a shuffling behind the tall grass. It could be a lion, or a warrior from an enemy tribe. In either case, you are in danger and will have to either fight or run. Or it could be a rabbit, in which case you will have to act quickly to secure tonight's dinner. Or it might be a wild boar, which is also potentially dinner, but might also be a threat if you are not quick and careful with his tusks. You don't have much time to determine whether the noise represents a crisis, an opportunity, or both, and within a fraction of a second your entire body has reoriented itself to prepare you for whatever the surprise might actually be.

Your brain directs various glands to release a complex chain reaction of hormones into your bloodstream that cause changes in your cells. Two of the most important stress hormones are adrenaline (also called epinephrine) and cortisol. These and other hormones unlock glucose, proteins, and fat stored in cells from food you've eaten and flush them into the bloodstream, where they can be used as energy by the muscles. They also interfere with insulin, whose job it is to remove glucose from the bloodstream and store it in your cells for later use.

Now that you have a massive energy supply flooding your bloodstream, you need to kick-start the circulatory system so that everything gets quickly transported where it needs to go. Stress hormones speed up the heart and lungs to supply more oxygen to the bloodstream and also cause the blood vessels to contract, which makes every heartbeat pump blood with greater force. Like water through a partially crimped hose, it turns from a stream to a spray as your blood pressure rises. Heart attacks are more likely to occur during these moments of stress, as it is then that the heart is working its hardest.

Another vital resource for your body in a potential crisis is water. Stress hormones tell your kidneys to stop taking water out of the bloodstream to make urine, while throughout the body water is diverted from tissues to the bloodstream, where it is available for use as needed. This explains why your mouth gets dry when you are about to make a wedding toast, just when you'd like to have a tongue that did not stick to the roof of your mouth.

Finally, your stress system triggers an immune response called inflammation. We ordinarily experience inflammation as a painful red swelling around a cut or insect bite. Or you feel it as the sore, scratchy feeling in your throat when you realize you're not just tired, you're coming down with a cold. The body is flooding the potentially infected tissues with immune cells, ready to kill invading organisms. The painful feeling that we experience as the infection is actually the body's reaction against it. It is the body's own cocktail of antibiotics and antivirals.

One of the leading roles in this assault is played by a kind of cell called a macrophage (which translates to "big eater"). Unlike other parts of the immune system that remember specific invaders and target them directly for destruction, inflammation's tactic is equivalent to a carpet bombing. These cells ask only one question: Is it me or not-me? If the answer is not-me (that is to say, if the molecular markers of one's own body are not detected), then the big eaters gobble it up.

We normally think of the immune system as reactive, in that once a bacterium or virus has infiltrated the body, it mounts a counterattack. That's true, but the stress response does not wait until the body's perimeter has actually been breached. As soon as the grass starts rustling, the body scrambles to prepare a preemptive response. Inflammatory cells are secreted into the bloodstream to be ready as a precaution.

This impressive crisis response system raises an important question: If our body has the power to boost our energy, deploy a preemptive immune shield, and make us faster to respond to a challenge, then why do we wait for a stressful situation to put these impressive abilities to use? Why don't we exploit them all the time?

The first reason is that in evolution, as in other areas of life, there is no such thing as a free lunch. Stress does not create new energy; it only redirects it: When the stress response gives a boost in one area, it has to take something away somewhere else. In the face of the potential emergency stirring in the grass, your body shuts down all unnecessary functions. The glucose and proteins that flood your bloodstream are now being taken away from long-term projects like cell division, maintenance, and repair and redirected to the muscles.

Digestion, for example, grinds to a halt because that is a long-term project that will be irrelevant if you don't survive the next few minutes. Growth processes also get shut down, which accounts for a condition known as "stress dwarfism." Children who experience prolonged periods of intense stress, like abuse or neglect, may have stunted growth even if their nutrition is adequate.

The second reason we can't enjoy stress's benefits all the time is that it causes terrible side effects. We are accustomed to thinking of the body's responses as natural and, therefore, not harmful to us. But the hormones released during stress are essentially powerful drugs made in-house. Doctors use adrenaline and cortisol (in its synthetic form, cortisone) and other stress hormones as medications for a variety of problems, but do so sparingly, however, because they have serious consequences. As with other drugs, our naturally produced stress hormones are safe if used only occasionally and for short periods. But that isn't the way we typically employ them.

Robert Sapolsky, a Stanford biologist and expert on stress, has argued that if we utilized our stress response the way other animals do, we would reap its benefits and avoid many of its costs. But it is the very qualities that make stress a brilliant power booster throughout the animal kingdom that also make it a cause of misery and disease for humans. As we have seen, the brilliance of stress is that it does not wait until there is actual tissue damage: It kicks in when faced with a potential threat. Humans, however, can sense a threat that is not actually physically present. Just spend a minute thinking about something that terrifies you or makes you anxious. Soon you will notice your heart beating faster. Your temperature may rise and you might start to sweat a bit. You are triggering your stress response merely with your thoughts. Unlike other animals, we humans have the ability to lie awake at night worrying about tomorrow's PowerPoint presentation, next month's mortgage payment, or a weird-looking mole on your back.

Also unlike other animals, humans can turn the stress response on for weeks, months, or years at a time. Think of the ramifications: We are exploiting a system that is designed to ignore long-term costs in order to redirect every resource to escaping an immediate emergency, but using it over the long term.

When stress hormones stop insulin from storing glucose for extended periods of time, we are at greater risk for diabetes and obesity. When they make the heart pump harder and the blood vessels constrict for months on end, we become prone to cardiovascular disease. And when inflammation goes unchecked, the immune system can become overactive—so eager to attack that it ceases to differentiate between cells that are "me" and "not-me." When the immune system starts to mount an offensive against our own body's cells, it causes autoimmune diseases.

Another way it can become overstimulated is by failing to differentiate between harmful invaders (bacteria and viruses) and harmless substances (like pollen, dust mites, or certain ingredients in foods). When that happens, an allergy develops. Long-term inflammation is also a risk factor for heart disease, depression, and other serious disorders.

None of this seems very adaptive, does it? We saw in Chapter 2 how our craving for status, like our appetites for food and sex, can get us in trouble because what worked well for millennia is not always suited to our modern environment. The same mismatch is true of stress. Recall that our ancestors were hunter-gatherers for much, much longer than we have lived as we do today. Archaeologists estimate that 15 percent of the population in prehistoric times died a violent death. That is five times higher than the comparable rate in the twentieth century, including all the deaths from both world wars, the Holocaust, and other genocides. Before modern sanitation and antibiotics, simple infections caused astronomical mortality rates. Life expectancy among the ancient Greeks, for example, was about thirty-five years. In the presence of so much violence and disease, with none of modern medicine's cures, the self-medication of stress provided the best shot at beating these acute threats of infection and injury. Today, the massive arsenal of our threat response system is the same, but the nature of the threats has changed.

Our ancestors could lie awake in their caves worrying about tomorrow just as we do. But for them, the downsides of stress were massively outweighed by its benefits. Unlike our ancestors, we are now fortunate to live long enough to succumb more often to the diseases of old age, rather than to predators in the grass. The downside of that trade is that the side effects of stress can be more harmful in the contemporary environment than the threats it evolved to protect us from. Today in economically developed countries, some of the most common causes of death are heart disease, stroke, and diabetes, all of which can be caused or worsened by stress. Now that fewer organisms are able to kill us, we are left with a cure that may be worse than the disease.

Because stress is the body's way of focusing on an immediate crisis at the expense of long-term costs, it's not surprising that economic hardship and low social status can lead to bodily stress reactions. Many different kinds of studies have confirmed the link between status and stress. Consider, for example, Robert Sapolsky's work with baboons living wild in a national park in Kenya. Sapolsky spent his summers observing the animals for years, getting to know individual members of their troops, and what rank each animal held in the hierarchy. To measure their stress, he would anaesthetize a baboon with a medicated dart and then take a blood sample. He found that the lower the baboon's rank in the pecking order, the higher its stress hormone levels and the more likely it was to suffer from stress-related illnesses such as ulcers. But high-ranking males, who could mate with any females they chose and take out aggression on any lower-ranking male, had much lower levels of stress.

One summer Sapolsky noticed that the baboons had taken to foraging in a garbage pit next to a tourist lodge. From the monkeys' point of view, it was an easy buffet. Of course, not all the baboons were allowed to enjoy the feast, as dominant males mainly kept the spoils for themselves, getting fat as they ate the junk food. Ironically, the baboons eating from the garbage pile contracted bovine tuberculosis, a disease they never would have been exposed to in their natural foraging grounds. Within three years, the more dominant males died off, leaving the troop with a hierarchy, but the most aggressive males were no longer at the head of it. When Sapolsky analyzed blood samples from the subordinate males in this newly flattened social order, he found lower levels of stress hormones.

Studies in laboratory monkeys have shown a correlation between having higher rank in the troop and having less bodily stress. But that correlation doesn't tell us whether it is low rank itself that causes increased stress or whether increased stress causes low rank. It might be that the anxious monkeys are the ones who are dominated by less stress-prone members of the troop. So researchers at Wake Forest University experimentally altered the hierarchy of monkeys living in laboratory-based troops to better understand cause and effect. First, they confirmed that, in a primate hierarchy, the lower down the social ladder an animal is, the higher its stress hormones will tend to be. They then did the lower-ranking monkeys a big favor by permanently removing the dominant ones from the troop.

The researchers found that if you remove the most dominant animals, the stress hormones of the "middle management" animals decrease, as they find themselves suddenly "promoted" by the absence of the boss. The laboratory experiments confirmed what Sapolsky suspected from his field research: Rank in the hierarchy is responsible for differences in levels of stress hormones, rather than the other way around.

Heightened stress responses in low-ranking primates makes biological sense, because it is the low-ranking animals who are most likely to be beaten, bitten, and deprived of their dinner. They need to mobilize their bodies' resources to deal with emergencies a lot more often than the alpha males do. Is this also true of humans? We don't exactly have dominance hierarchies, but we do have plenty of hierarchical structures just the same. We measure them not with food and mating rights, but with money, power, social class, and social comparison. Based on the animal research, we should expect that individuals of lower status should be more stressed than others.

Indeed, studies have shown that people with lower incomes tend to have higher levels of stress hormones, like cortisol and adrenaline, in their bloodstreams. They tend to have hyperreactive immune systems and higher levels of inflammation in particular. Some studies have measured stress hormones and inflammation as people go about their daily business, and found that those who are poorer or who feel lower in status have slightly higher levels. But the differences really ramp up if you expose individuals to stress and see how their bodies react.

One study by Andrew Steptoe at University College London recruited volunteers from high- and low-status occupations within the British Civil Service and gave them stressful tasks to do. In one experiment, subjects had to use a pen to trace a moving star on a computer screen. That sounds easy, but the subjects could only see their hand through a mirror, so right appeared as left and vice versa. The experiment was designed so that the star moved quickly enough that the subjects would make mistakes, and the computer beeped loudly whenever the pen veered off the path. To guarantee the task would be stressful, the experimenters told the subjects that "the average person" could trace the star accurately, implying that the inevitable errors would leave them feeling less than average.

During and after the star-tracing task, the experimenters measured subjects' heart rate and markers of inflammation in their blood. Both high- and low-status groups rated the task as equally stressful. But their bodies reacted differently. The low-status group showed more inflammation markers in their bloodstream. And although both groups had higher heart rates during the test, those of the high-status group soon returned to normal. The low-status group was still showing elevated rates two hours later.

A continent away in Los Angeles, psychologist Keely Muscatell and colleagues obtained similar results using a completely different method, and added a fascinating new wrinkle. This study began by interviewing volunteers while video-recording them. Imagine what it's like to be a subject in this study: You go to a lab at UCLA, where you fill out a questionnaire, including information about your income and your position on the Status Ladder. You are then interviewed by a pleasant, professional college student, who asks personal questions like: What are you most proud of in your life? What would you most like to change about yourself?

The following day you go to a laboratory where a nurse places a needle in your arm to sample your blood, and then lie down in an fMRI machine to have your brain scanned. The device looks like a hospital bed, except that you place your head in the center of a white donut-like structure. It is made of smooth plastic, like the overhead baggage compartments in an airplane, and is the size of a Volkswagen. As you take your position, you look up at a little computer screen inside the donut hole and learn that another experimental subject is going to watch the interview you just recorded and rate what she thinks of you. And you get to watch her ratings. On a little computer screen appears a grid of squares, and within each square is a personality description. As the other subject watches your video, she moves a cursor around the screen, effectively complimenting or insulting you with her clicks. One minute she thinks you're—click—*intelligent*. The next, she decides you are—click—*annoying*. How rude! A moment later, she sees the real you again—click—*caring*. The process goes on for a while, but what you didn't know is that the "subject" in the other room was a sham, and it was the experimenters who were systematically praising and insulting you with those mouse clicks while scanning your brain and monitoring your blood throughout the emotional roller-coaster ride.

The researchers found that when volunteers were being evaluated by the person in the other room, markers of inflammation in their blood rose significantly. This effect was especially powerful for those who rated themselves as low on the Status Ladder: Their inflammation spiked.

There are several striking things about these findings. First, we have experimental evidence that the social evaluation actually caused the changes in inflammation, not simply that the two are correlated. Second, the whole process took place over the course of about ninety minutes, and inflammatory changes were detected in less than an hour. The human social hierarchy was playing out and expressing itself throughout nearly every cell in the body on a scale of minutes.

The study made one more startling discovery. The pathway from subjective ratings of status to inflammation in the bloodstream was controlled by brain activity in a particular network of regions in the frontal cortex. These regions are activated, among other things, when people think about the thoughts, feelings, and perspectives of others. Although more research is needed to confirm this initial finding and its interpretation, the authors suggest that the brain may be actively computing where we fall along the Status Ladder using the same neural machinery we ordinarily use to assess what other people are thinking of us. Like Sapolsky's baboons, humans in this study were reacting to a low rank in the hierarchy as if it were a physical threat. Their bodies mobilized an immune response as if social slights were literal attacks.

For public relations firms or emergency medical responders or biological organisms, there is only one way to manage a crisis: to prioritize immediate necessities and deal with the future later. There may, of course, have been organisms that took a different approach. But the ones who ignored the most pressing demands in a critical situation are no longer with us to share their wisdom. Tending to immediate needs at the expense of the future is what your brain is doing when it dumps cortisol and adrenaline into the bloodstream. It is unleashing the energy and inflammation that ready you for battle, and if it risks diabetes and heart disease one day, then so be it. That is what your brain is doing when it tunes attention to the rustling in the bushes and ignores everything in the background. When you feel that you have nothing, even the cells in your body start demanding to take what they need now and worry about the future later. Inequality accelerates this process by making everyone feel less secure. It does not matter whether we measure the effects in dry mortality statistics or in the faded granite of a tombstone. Eventually we pay the price for this crisis management, as the future becomes now and our later becomes sooner.

Chapter 6

God, Conspiracies, and the Language of the Angels

Why People Believe What They Need to Believe

What would you do with $28,000? Buy a new car? Put a down payment on a house? Pay off student loans? Fortunately for Diane Duyser of Fort Lauderdale, someone chose to spend his $28,000 on Diane's grilled cheese sandwich. It wasn't just any sandwich, though—this one had the face of the Virgin Mary on it. It turns out that these kinds of apparitions are everywhere. Villagers in Russia worship the image of Jesus in the bark of a birch tree. A Welsh family saw Christ in a smear of Marmite stuck to the lid of the jar. And a New York man found the Lord in his navel orange. In recent years the Holy Family has made appearances in Cheetos, pretzels, Funyuns, and breakfast tacos. It was no grilled cheese, but the Funyun sold for $600.

This tendency to see patterns in randomness is called pareidolia. It's not a new phenomenon. David Hume noted in the eighteenth century that "there is an universal tendency among mankind to conceive all beings like themselves, and to transfer to every object, those qualities, with which they are familiarly acquainted . . . We find human faces in the moon, armies in the clouds; and by a natural propensity, if not corrected by experience and reflection, ascribe malice or good-will to every thing, that hurts or pleases us."

Figure 6.1. How easily you see a face in this cloud depends on your needs at the moment. Wanda Hartwigsen/National Oceanic and Atmospheric Administration/Department of Commerce

Why, exactly, do people have this "universal tendency" to see deities in their snack foods? As we will learn, these visions have less to do with the spirit world than with the minds of the individuals who experience them. But these people are not crazy. On the contrary, they are engaging in an activity that we all do every day, one that brings order and sanity to our lives. Randomness and chaos feel threatening, but orderly patterns are reassuring, helping us feel that the world is predictable, trustworthy, and controllable. When people detect patterns in noise, they are extracting meaning from a world that has too few bright lines and too many gray areas. Of course, we do not see just any patterns. Faces are especially common, because faces are especially informative to us, and the faces of religious icons are even more evocative. When a sense of meaning is what we are looking for, we tend toward the epic. The ancient Greeks looked up at the stars and saw constellations of gods and heroes, not errand boys.

We ordinarily think that our perceptions of the things around us are driven simply by the things themselves. And we normally assume that our beliefs about the world are driven by the world itself. But both our perceptions and beliefs are also driven by our needs and desires at any moment. For example, food tastes better when we are hungry, heat feels better when we are cold, and certain stories seem truer when we really need an explanation. In this chapter we'll explore how inequalities in power, wealth, and social status change our perceptions of reality, our religious experiences, and the beliefs we hold dear. All of us want to live in a world that is stable and predictable, where someone is in control, and where chaos can be tamed. All of us want to live in a world of justice, where good things happen to good people and bad people are punished for their crimes. Our minds are working hard at every moment tidying up the world, but inequality plods through the door with muddy shoes, bringing disorder in its wake.

A key point to understand is that the human brain is a pattern detector. The visual system, for example, receives a constantly shifting barrage of light and color and motion, and tries to construct a stable three-dimensional image of the world from it. The brain is remarkably effective at this task, and is light-years ahead of even the best artificial intelligence systems currently available. The reason is not that the eyes are such finely calibrated sensors (digital cameras can in some respects "see" more than the eye), but rather that the brain is better at making inferences, leaps of logic, and filling in gaps based on assumptions.

You can catch your brain in the process of filling in these gaps, because the human eye has a design quirk that creates a major problem for vision. The retina is the layer of photoreceptors that covers the back of your eyeball and converts light into neural signals. The signals are carried by the optic nerve, which passes through the back of the eyeball to the brain. But the place where the optic nerve exits the eyeball leaves a patch with no photoreceptors, creating a blind spot in each eye. We don't ordinarily notice this flaw because the brain takes the image from one eye and "fills in" what we "should" be seeing from the other. As long as one eye can see the parts that the other misses, we never notice the hole in the world.

You may have seen a figure like the one below used to illustrate the existence of the blind spot. But I want to use it to demonstrate how the brain fills in perceptual gaps. First, cover your left eye. Then, with your right eye, focus on the cross. Move the page slowly closer and farther from your face while keeping focused on the cross.

You should notice two things. First, at a certain distance, the dot will disappear, revealing your blind spot. Because you have covered your left eye, it can no longer supply the material that would ordinarily be employed to fill in the scene. But even more important, you will notice that, when the dot disappears, the box is immediately filled in with gray. Even though your left eye can't tip off the right eye about the dot, portions of the right eye can still see the gray box. And so, the brain does the best it can and papers over the box with more of the same.

Now you can switch eyes. Cover your right eye and focus on the dot this time. This time, when the cross vanishes, the space is filled in with white. Even for an action as basic as perceiving light and dark, the brain makes assumptions to fill in gaps. It assumes that the world is not random; that even if it has only partial

Figure 6.2. Your vision system fills in blind spots using assumptions from the context.

knowledge, it can safely guess what is missing because the world is an orderly and predictable place.

This assumption that the world is orderly and predictable is a kind of mental bedrock that forms the foundation for all of our perception, thinking, and believing. We are so good at generating regular patterns that it can at times interfere with our ability to recognize when no pattern exists at all. Imagine you buy a lottery ticket and choose six numbers. Which of the two number sequences is more likely to be drawn by chance: 1 2 3 4 5 6, or 43 7 17 38 9 24? The answer is that both sequences are equally likely. They don't *look* equally likely, though, because we can easily discern a pattern in the first one, and a pattern seems like the opposite of randomness.

The Internet is full of discussions about how to pick winning lottery numbers. Richard Lustig, who has won lotteries seven times, recommends choosing your own numbers rather than relying on the automatic "Quick Pick." Internet commenters chimed in to recommend using personally meaningful dates, whereas others cautioned strictly against doing so. One person suggested that "using a lottery numbers generator will also increase your odds of winning the lottery because your numbers are picked purely at random JUST LIKE the lottery machine does." But all of these recommendations misunderstand the nature of randomness. The definition of a random draw is that any number has an equal chance of appearing. It does not matter if they are generated by you, a machine, or your favorite uncle. It does not matter if the numbers are as arbitrary as your first phone number or as sacred as the date your mother died. Randomness means there is no cause and effect. There is no correlation between what you do to pick numbers and what numbers come up. There is no pattern, and no order. The numbers are utterly devoid of meaning, other than denoting the winner.

If my claim that there is no rhyme or reason to lottery numbers feels a little depressing, then you can begin to appreciate how closely we connect pattern to our emotional need to find meaning. Patterns are comfortable, so even when the topic is a purely random numerical process, insisting that there is no underlying order or larger meaning can feel a little like bullying.

The tendency to find meaningful patterns in randomness is universal, as Hume argued, but it happens more in some circumstances than others. We are especially likely to manufacture meaningful patterns when we feel powerless. The predictability, and therefore controllability, of patterns provides a bit of solace from the lack of control. This might help explain why it never seems to be the Volvo-driving accountant who sees Jesus in his cinnamon toast.

Psychologists Jennifer Whitson and Adam Galinsky directly tested the relationship between powerlessness and pareidolia in a series of experiments. In one condition, the researchers made subjects feel momentarily powerless by asking them to tell a detailed story to relive a time when something happened to them that made them feel a complete lack of control. Another group told about a time when they felt completely in control. Subjects then viewed pictures of random black-and-white "static," were told that some of the images contained a hidden picture, and were asked to identify which ones they were. The images were in fact pure noise, but the "powerless" subjects were about three times more likely to see a picture hidden in the static. The transient feeling of helplessness made their brains work a little harder to extract meaning from nonsense.

Research by psychologist Nick Epley and colleagues has found that when people feel left out, left behind, or socially disconnected, they may also start to anthropomorphize the things around them. Their dogs and cats seem as relatable as people. Gods, ghosts, and demons seem like real entities. Even an inanimate object like an alarm clock can feel like a sentient being that is intent on being annoying.

Seeing people in clouds, clocks, or cheese sandwiches is one way to impose order on chaos, but it is not the most common one. A more typical method we use to find meaning in our lives is to spin stories about the world around us. The most effective are those that make everything seem to fit together in a way that we can understand, but some of the most satisfying of them have the unfortunate property of being very unlikely to be true.

Recently a pollster asked more than 1,200 Americans about their beliefs on a variety of issues. Twenty-eight percent believed that a mysterious power elite with a globalist agenda is conspiring to rule the world through an authoritarian New World Order. The New World Order is a conspiracy theory linked to the Illuminati, a secret society claimed to run other organizations, like the Free-masons, the Hollywood movie industry, and the United States government. In some accounts, the organization is also known as SPECTRE, the cabal of supervillains in James Bond books and movies. Twenty-eight percent! If that percentage of conspiracy theorists is extrapolated to the entire population of this country, it amounts to about eighty-eight million Americans.

The same poll found that twenty-one percent of respondents believed that an alien UFO crashed in Roswell, New Mexico, and that the government had covered the incident up. Fifty-one percent believed that the assassination of John F. Kennedy was a conspiracy rather than the work of a lone gunman. Thirty-seven percent believed that global warming is a hoax, and fifteen percent believed that the pharmaceutical industry is in league with the medical industry to invent new diseases to make money. Four percent (about twelve million Americans) believe that "shape-shifting reptilian people control our world by taking on human form and gaining political power to manipulate our societies."

All told, about half of Americans believe in some form of conspiracy theory, and that proportion has remained roughly constant across decades. The particular forms these theories take come and go. Conspiracy theories have often been widely circulated, full of anger and outrage, only to be inevitably forgotten about. Around the time of the American Civil War, one widespread conspiracy theory in the North held that a secret cabal of powerful men from slaveholding states called the Slave Power was secretly assassinating Union government officials.

At bottom, conspiracy theories are about two things: power and distrust. You can see the former at work in who believes which theories about whom. The best predictor of which conspiracy theories people believe at any given time is which political party is in power. The same poll I described above found that Democrats were more likely than Republicans to believe that the U.S. government (led by George W. Bush) allowed the 9/11 terrorist attacks to happen. Under Barack Obama's administration, different conspiracies abounded, claiming that he was not born in America, he is a secret Muslim, and so on. They are believed mainly by the right. People who feel powerless tend to believe in conspiracies carried out by the powerful.

Whitson and Galinsky investigated the link between power and conspiracy theories with the same methods they used to study power and pareidolia. They conducted an experiment that made one group of subjects feel powerless and another feel powerful. They then showed both groups several paranoid, conspiracy-based explanations for everyday events and asked how plausible they seemed. The group that had been made to feel powerless found the conspiracy explanations more believable than the group that felt powerful. This experiment established some of the first cause-and-effect evidence for the reasons people believe in conspiracies. It's not just that the powerless people happen to believe more in such theories because of some individual characteristic, like intelligence, education, or personal tastes. Instead, it's the particular circumstances in which people find themselves that can be a motivating factor.

A study by psychologist Michael Wood and colleagues examined two conspiracy theories about the killing of Osama bin Laden under the Obama administration. One theory holds that American SEAL Team Six did not really kill Bin Laden, who was actually dead long before the troops ever raided his compound in Abbottabad, Pakistan; the raid was simply staged so that President Obama could take credit for killing the terrorist leader. The second theory holds that Bin Laden was never killed but remains alive today, secretly running al-Qaeda and plotting new attacks.

Wood found, curiously, that people who believed more strongly in the first theory were also more likely to believe in the second, even though, logically, Bin Laden could hardly have been dead before the raid that supposedly killed him and also still alive. The common element, the researchers found, was distrust of government authorities: Those who thought that people in power were likely to deceive the public with a cover-up were more likely to accept both theories. Distrust—not facts or logic—made even contradictory theories seem more plausible than the official account. To believe in a conspiracy, you trade a bit of your belief that the world is good, fair, and just in exchange for the conviction that at least someone—anyone—has everything under control.

But it's not necessary to abandon one's faith in a just world. One of the simplest ways that people maintain the sense that the world is orderly is merely to insist that it is so, and then backfill their reasoning to make everything add up. Many years ago psychologist Mel Lerner made this point by orchestrating an elaborate experiment. In one laboratory room a young woman sat at a desk with wires and electrodes hooked up to her. She was taking a learning and memory test, listening to questions from the experimenter and answering them. Whenever she made mistakes—and she made a lot of mistakes—the experimenter administered a shock. The scene was dramatic: She screamed; she cried. And yet the experiment continued relentlessly, session after session.

In reality, the young woman was an actor receiving fake shocks. The real subjects in this experiment were on the other side of a see-through mirror, watching the scientifically sanitized torment unfold. They were asked to observe the "learner" and rate the emotions that she appeared to be experiencing from one moment to the next. After ten minutes of shocks, one group was told that there would now be a break, after which the "learning" would be resumed. Another group of participants was told that the shocks would be stopped, and after the break the young woman would be compensated with money for the pain she had endured. Then, almost as an afterthought, subjects were asked to rate their impressions of the young woman. In fact, it was these impressions that the researchers were interested in all along.

For the group who believed that the woman was going to be compensated for her suffering, the world remained a just place. Yes, she had suffered from the shocks, but the remuneration would even the scales. But for the group who thought the senseless torment was going to resume, the situation seemed absurd and unjust. This poor subject was suffering for the sake of a silly study, and the observers had every reason to feel sympathetic toward the poor victim. And yet, they deplored her. The group who thought she was going to continue suffering called her unlikable and immature. They said it would be hard to admire or respect someone like her and that they would not like to get to know her. This was exactly what Lerner had predicted would happen. In order to maintain the certitude that the world was fair, subjects manufactured flaws in the woman's character. Just as your visual system fills in the scene with assumptions to render the world sensible, so does your moral reasoning. Good things happen to good people, and bad things happen to bad people.

Something bad is happening to this woman. Therefore, she must be a bad person. All is well.

We see the same mental gymnastics when people try to explain why some individuals earn a lot of money and others don't. In another of Lerner's experiments, he had two people solving puzzles at a table, with subjects again watching the session unfold through a see-through mirror. The experimenter then explained that he had money to pay only one of the puzzlers. He drew a name out of a hat and paid the lucky winner, while the loser went home empty-handed. Even though they had just seen that the name was drawn randomly, subjects believed that the winner had worked harder, made a greater contribution, and was more creative in his puzzle solutions than the loser. The certainty that we get what we deserve, and deserve what we get, was so powerful that it overrode the evidence of their senses telling people that the outcome was a matter of random chance.

Our tendency to mentally contort our way toward justice applies also to ourselves. Inspired by Lerner's experiments, economist Jeffrey Butler recently asked whether being highly paid made people think more highly of themselves. To test this idea, he had groups of research subjects complete a test of logical reasoning. Within each group, one half were told that they would be paid four dollars for each correct answer, and the other half were told that they would be paid only two dollars. Just as in Lerner's experiment, the researchers openly informed the subjects that the choice of who got which pay rate was entirely random. After answering ten questions, subjects were asked to rate their own reasoning abilities. Even though the highly paid subjects did not perform any better on the reasoning test, they perceived themselves as superior reasoners and harder workers than the low-pay subjects. Perhaps more surprising was the fact that the low-pay workers agreed, rating themselves as less proficient as well.

In the real world, where success and failure are driven by a complex blend of talent, effort, and chance, we are even more disposed to assume that people get what they deserve. For those on the losing end, that assumption is against their self-interest, but it still serves a purpose: It helps reassure them that the world is not utterly chaotic. The system may not be working for them, but at least there *is* a system.

Most people don't stop with the assumption that the world is a just place. It is just because it is in the hands of someone who is just. Monotheistic religions provide believers with the reassurance that a benevolent, all-knowing, and all-powerful being is controlling the universe. This type of belief system offers many benefits. Unlike conspiracy theories, which provide controllability but at the expense of benevolence, religious belief is the ultimate win-win.

The science concerning the psychological origins and consequences of religious belief applies equally whether those beliefs are themselves true or false. And it applies equally to Christians, Muslims, Jews, and Hindus, who believe mutually exclusive things about God. Explaining the psychological reasons for belief and disbelief does not necessarily imply that there is no God, just as explaining why believers get certain emotional benefits compared with nonbelievers does not imply that God exists. As Voltaire said, "If God did not exist, it would be necessary to invent him."

If feeling powerless and insecure makes people more prone to see patterns and to give credence to conspiracy theories, it stands to reason that it would also intensify religious faith. Studies by Aaron Kay have confirmed that when individuals are made to feel helpless or when the world is portrayed as chaotic and unpredictable, they hold stronger convictions in a powerful God who controls the universe. Believers often console themselves with slogans like "Let go and let God" and "Everything happens for a reason." Feeling powerless magnifies the appeal of these notions.

In another study, psychologists Kurt Gray and Daniel Wegner looked at the U.S. states where people had more or fewer hardships in their lives by compiling statistics on infant mortality, cancer deaths, infectious disease, violent crime, and environmental hazards. They combined these maladies into a single "suffering index" and plotted it against the proportion of people in each state who stated in polls that they strongly believed in God. Many theologians find suffering to pose a philosophical problem for religion, because it seems contradictory that a God who is all-powerful, all-good, and all-knowing would allow such misery. But the researchers found that anguish does not pose a theological problem for most believers. Quite the opposite. Like the biblical Job, the more people suffered, the more they had faith in God.

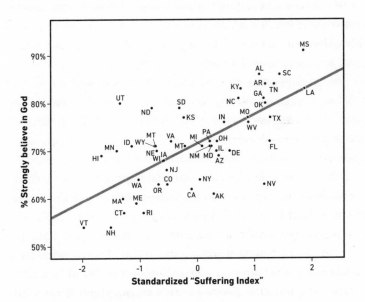

Figure 6.3. States where people suffer more have stronger belief in God. From Gray and Wegner, 2010.

This finding supports the idea that as societies become wealthier and more economically advanced, religion will begin to decline. This idea was almost universally embraced by the great intellectuals of the nineteenth century. Karl Marx, Sigmund Freud, and Émile Durkheim couldn't have been more different in their thinking, yet all agreed that as the ideas of the Renaissance and the progress of the industrial revolution took root, religion would diminish and scientific theories like evolution would replace beliefs like creationism. Germ theory would supplant sin and demonic possession as the cause of disease. The authority of spiritual healers and shamans would be ceded to physicians as modern medicine gave humans control over diseases that had afflicted them for millennia. Technology, from modern farming to air-conditioning, would make life less fragile before the whims of nature. Cosmology would replace mythology in our search to understand how the universe works, and for our own origins. And all of these changes together would encourage the pursuit of reason and evidence as the surest way to answer life's big questions and solve everyday problems.

By the mid-twentieth century, this secularization theory was taken as an article of faith. In 1968 sociologist Peter Berger told the *New York Times*, "By the 21st century, religious believers are likely to be found only in small sects, huddled together to resist a worldwide secular culture . . . The predicament of the believer is increasingly like that of a Tibetan astrologer on a prolonged visit to an American university." Empowered by the Enlightenment, mankind would no longer long for God.

Has the prediction of the intellectuals come to pass? No, and yes. No, in the sense that most of the world remains clearly, obviously, and deeply religious. Surveys suggest that about 84 percent of the world's 7 billion people profess a religious faith. But this may not reflect a failure of the theory that science would replace religion so much as a failure to predict how unevenly economic and

Wealthier Nations Tend to Be Less Religious, But U.S. a Prominent Exception
% saying religion plays a very important role in their lives (2011–2013)

Figure 6.4. Wealthier countries tend to be less religious. Data from Pew Research Center.

scientific development would spread around the world. There are many places today where daily life has no resemblance at all to the university that Berger envisioned.

So, are economically developed countries less religious than poor ones? Here, the answer is clearly yes. As you can see in polling data in Figure 6.4, the wealthier the country, the less important religion is to the average citizen. The same trends can be seen if we look at other measures, like frequency of church attendance or the proportion of people who believe in God. Upwards of 90 percent of the population in very poor countries like Pakistan and Nigeria say that religion is very important in their lives. But the self-identified religious number only around 20 percent in wealthy Canada, Australia, and Germany. This appears to be clear confirmation that as people's lives become more secure in material terms, they have less need for the consolations of religion.

Yet there are two clear outliers to this pattern, one of which is easy to explain and the other of which is not. The former is China, where the communist government actively suppressed religion for decades. It's no surprise that religion would be less important than predicted from the nation's average income. The more puzzling exception is the highly religious United States. Despite having by far the highest income per capita in the survey, its measure of religious belief is on par with that of Mexico, Lebanon, and South Africa.

Of course, the prevalence of religion depends on many factors beyond income, like a country's particular history and culture. America, for example, was founded in part by immigrants seeking refuge from religious persecution, which surely accounts for some of its unusual levels of devoutness. Recent research, however, suggests another, more powerful explanation. Using the most extensive database available, political scientist Frederick Solt examined the level of religious belief across countries and was able to explain both the general trends and the outliers. After accounting for the difference between communist and noncommunist countries, China was no longer an outlier. Even more important, though, was the role of income inequality. Highly unequal countries were much more religious than more equal ones. The effects of inequality were huge, and about as large as the effects of actual income. Once the data were plotted to show the relationship between religion and income inequality (rather than average income), the United States was no longer an outlier but fell right along the line where it would be expected to be, high in both inequality and religiosity. Poverty and inequality together can explain the bulk of the differences across countries in religiosity.

Although no research has yet firmly established why inequality and religion are linked, I predict that when the research is done, the key factor will be inner feelings of status and security. We have already seen in Chapter 2 that the average person feels poorer and lower in status in highly unequal places. We have also learned in this chapter that when people feel powerless or left out, they are more likely to attach themselves to belief systems that make the world seem fair, predictable, and meaningful. It does not take a big leap to imagine that when inequality rises, everyone feels less secure and religion looks more appealing. Notice that this trend has nothing to do with the specific beliefs of any particular religion. In predominantly Christian countries, inequality is linked to greater belief in Jesus; in predominantly Muslim countries, inequality is linked to greater belief in Mohammed, and so on. People tend to turn to whatever belief system they were raised with when they feel insecure in the world.

Secularists are fond of pointing out logical inconsistencies in sacred writings, the improbable nature of miracles, and the impossibility of proving the supernatural. But many religion scholars have countered that, for most believers, facts and logic are not at the root of belief. Religion is not a coherent set of propositions that are either true or false, the way a scientific theory is. Instead, many people believe because of their personal subjective experiences. These might include the awe and wonder of nature, the intimacy of belonging to a close community, or the comforting experience of hearing God speak to you in a familiar voice. Those feelings are the product of emotions and social relationships, not theology.

The poor are not only more religious than the affluent; they are religious in different ways. People with low incomes are more likely to believe that the Bible is the literal word of God, as opposed to a divinely inspired general set of teachings. The poor are more likely to believe in miracles, in faith healing, and in demonic possession.

Growing up in Kentucky, I lived with exactly the combination of low incomes and high inequality that would predict intense religious beliefs. In fact, my community was a world full of miracles and mysteries. I once saw an earnest teenager slain in the spirit. When the pastor lightly touched her forehead, she became so full of fervor from the Holy Spirit, she would later explain, that she fell limp to the floor. Another girl convulsed as if attached to an invisible high-voltage wire.

As a child, I once pestered a family member to show me how she spoke in tongues. She explained that if you prayed to God, He would send the Holy Spirit to you and you would be moved to speak in strange languages. They might be foreign earthly languages, or they might be languages known only to the angels. My relative's speech sounded like a mix of Latin and Italian, though I had hoped for something more celestial.

Charismatic religious communities teach their children how to experience God on a personal level. One beautiful spring day the pastor of my religious school took our class outside for an unusual lesson. We sat down in the grass next to a small garden with yellow lilies and tall grasses swaying in a warm breeze. He proceeded to give us a lesson based on the familiar Bible verse: "Look at the birds of the air: they neither sow nor reap nor gather into barns, and yet your heavenly Father feeds them. Are you not of more value than they? . . . Consider the lilies of the field, how they grow: they neither toil nor spin, yet I tell you, even Solomon in all his glory was not arrayed like one of these." He told us that if we closed our eyes and felt the wind and listened to the rustling of the grass, we would hear God's voice speaking to us through them.

I didn't sense anything but wind and grass, so I closed my eyes tighter and strained harder to hear. The wind sounded like a parent gently shushing a child. And then I heard it, clear as a bell: A voice said, "Peace, be still. I will always take care of you." It was electric. I was so thrilled that I couldn't pay attention to anything else at school for the rest of the day. That afternoon on the bus ride home, I kept replaying the voice in my head, trying to recapture the magic of that moment.

Then something occurred to me. The sentence I heard was actually a combination of two Bible verses that we had studied recently. In one, Jesus orders the sea to be calm, and it obeys; the other was a paraphrase of the verse about sparrows and lilies. My pastor had suggested a particular set of comforting thoughts to us, and then directed our attention to the wind and grass and urged us to listen for God's voice. How did I know that the voice was God's rather than an expression of my own thoughts?

So I tried a little experiment. I came up with a word—say, "purple." Then I closed my eyes and strained to hear the word in the din of the bus full of chattering children. Sure enough, I soon heard it. Had one of the children really said it, or had my mind fashioned it out of the thousand syllables flying past me? After I carried out this exercise with a few other words, I realized that if you try to hear something amid a cacophony of noise, then you are likely to hear it. "Transylvania?" I heard it. "Rutabaga?" I heard it. Maybe I was doing it wrong, but I didn't seem to have a head for miracles.

Years later I would understand that what I experienced that day was what the brain does when it sculpts a grilled cheese into the image of the Virgin or stitches together a dozen random happenings into a grand conspiracy. We all do this to one extent or another. But when people feel that they are being left behind, that life is chaotic and their position is precarious, their brain picks up the pace in its work of steadying the world. And the method works. Individuals who are religious tend to be happier and less anxious—about both life and death—than those who are not. Some belief systems provide comfort and reassurance in ways that ordinary thinking cannot. For most people, the abstract impersonal God of academic theologians cannot provide this level of comfort. The harder life is, the more miraculous it becomes.

Chapter 7

Inequality in Black and White

The Dangerous Dance of Racial and Economic Inequality

My first brush with race is not so much a memory as a story retold often enough to have the feel of one. I would have been four or five years old, in a grocery store with my mother. There was not much diversity in Maceo, Kentucky, so when a very tall African American man walked down the aisle, he may have been the first black person I had seen outside of TV. Maybe I was impressed with his stature. Maybe I was astonished by the color of his skin. But when I announced for the whole store to hear, "Hey, Momma, look at the great big—" no one would ever know how I finished the sentence, because Momma's hand had clapped so tightly over my mouth that not even the shape of the mumble that followed could be made out. Would I really have used a racial slur, or would I have simply called him a man? My mother wasn't taking any chances, and her quick reflexes were revealing.

When adults express a prejudice, you can point your finger at them and label them racist, sexist, xenophobic. But when a child does so, all we can do is listen with embarrassment. Children hold up a mirror to the society in which they are raised, so when we hear them utter a racial slur, we feel sad for humanity. What does it say about a culture in which a mother has to worry that her preschooler will use such terms? What does it say that the child just might do so?

Racial inequality is qualitatively different from income inequality. Rich and poor exist among all racial groups, and racial discrimination affects the lives of African Americans and other minority groups even when they are not poor. Although racial and economic inequalities are separate issues, they have been intersecting more and more often in recent years, as racial inequality stumbles ever so slowly downward and income inequality steadily rises. In this chapter we will discuss how widening income inequality throws fuel on the fires of racial prejudice and how racial stereotypes are used to justify and preserve that inequality.

Racial discrimination has, of course, been a part of America since the first slave ship reached North America at the English colony of Jamestown in 1619. Slavery built what would eventually become the United States. The institution lasted two and a half centuries, longer than the country itself has existed as of today. When slavery was ended in 1865, a system of Jim Crow laws took its place and kept African Americans legally oppressed for another full century. When the Civil Rights Act of 1964 outlawed overt racial discrimination, and the Voting Rights Act of 1965 ended explicitly discriminatory voting practices, society did not change overnight in response. Following that 350-year period of perfectly legal subjugation, a mere half century—less than a single lifetime—separates us from whites-only lunch counters, water fountains, and schools. How much have things changed since then? It depends whom you ask.

If you look at polls, the proportion of Americans favoring overtly racist ideas like segregated schools and hiring discrimination has declined from clear majorities in the 1960s to single digits today. These trends have been regarded as an encouraging sign, but perhaps we have drawn too much encouragement from them.

A 2011 survey asked a nationally representative sample of white

Racial, Ethnic Wealth Gaps Have Grown Since Great Recession
Median net worth of households, in 2013 dollars

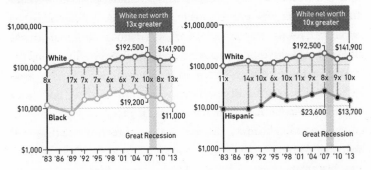

Notes: Blacks and whites include only non-Hispanics. Hispanics are of any race. Chart scale is logarithmic; each gridline is ten times greater than the gridline below it. Great Recession began Dec. '07 and ended June '09.

Figure 7.1. Wealth gaps between white Americans and black and Hispanic Americans have not closed in recent decades. Data from Pew Research Center.

and black Americans to rate how much they thought both blacks and whites were targets of discrimination in each decade from the 1950s to the 2000s. Both groups of respondents agreed that antiblack discrimination had decreased during the course of those decades, although whites thought that it had fallen much more steeply than blacks did. The two groups differed even more strikingly, though, in their perceptions of antiwhite discrimination. Black respondents thought antiwhite bias was not a problem in the 1950s and was still not a problem today. White respondents, in contrast, believed that antiwhite bias had steadily risen in the period in question. Whites seemed to view discrimination as a zero-sum game: The less discrimination they perceived against blacks, the more they saw it turned against whites. The trend was so stark in the eyes of white respondents that by the 2000s they judged discrimination against whites to be a bigger problem than discrimination against blacks.

The data, however, tell a very different story. The income gap between white and black families has remained more or less constant since the 1960s. In 1967 the average black family earned 55 percent of what white families earned. In 2011 that figure was 59 percent. Although the gaps between black and white families have narrowed for high school graduation rates and more modestly for college graduation, those improvements have not translated into a lessening of the income gaps.

Even more dramatic, racial gaps in wealth (i.e., total net worth) have only increased in recent decades. In 2013 white families had thirteen times the wealth of average black families and ten times the wealth of Hispanic families. This disparity is just as large as it was in the 1980s, and represents a step backward from the modestly narrower gaps in the 1990s. Something is preventing gains in education from translating into reduced income and wealth gaps.

One factor is home ownership, which is much higher for white families. A second, closely related factor is inheritance. Once a family has accumulated some wealth, it can be used for buying a home or establishing other assets for the next generation. But in black and Latino families, where the average wealth is close to zero, each generation starts essentially from scratch. Economists have identified several other factors that contribute to wealth gaps, including differences in incarceration rates and marriage and divorce rates. But it is impossible to understand these disparities without also understanding the role of racial discrimination, which creates a constant set of pressures on minority families.

These imbalances in wealth, education, and home ownership can serve as a kind of Rorschach test. If you believe that minority families are themselves to blame for their fates, then you can view these data as proof of it. And if you think minority families are the victims of discrimination and a systematic lack of opportunity, you can find support for that theory in the numbers as well. The problem is that the role of discrimination is very hard to isolate using statistics like the ones above. Data on average wealth or home ownership can tell us that disparities exist, but they can't explain why. For that, we need to turn to people's behavior.

In one groundbreaking experiment, sociologist Devah Pager tested for real-life discrimination by sending pairs of young men—one white and one black—to apply for jobs in Milwaukee. She gave them identical fabricated résumés so that they would have the same qualifications. She also provided the same scripts to use when introducing themselves and completing job applications. The pairs then applied to 350 jobs. They did not both apply for the same positions; which subject applied to each job was selected randomly, creating a randomized experiment. Then, like all job applicants, they waited for a call from the employers.

Did the results support the antiwhite bias that the "zero-sum" survey respondents believed existed? Not even close. The white applicant was called back twice as often as the equally qualified black applicant. Similar studies have been repeated with the same results in New York, Chicago, Atlanta, and other cities. They have also been replicated in areas other than employment. Black renters are much more likely than equally qualified white renters to be told there are no vacant apartments. Black shoppers are offered less favorable deals on cars and higher interest rates on mortgages than equally qualified whites. Antiblack bias is alive and well in twenty-first-century America.

If survey responses do not paint an accurate picture of racial attitudes today, there is another place we can look to find one. In the 1940s, a husband-and-wife team of psychologists, Kenneth and Mamie Clark, were among the first to realize that if you want to gauge how society's values and expectations seep into our minds, you should look at the minds of children, the best cultural sponges we have. The Clarks were remarkable not only for their trailblazing research, but also for the fact that they were African American scholars working at a time when most universities would not let blacks enter through the same doors as whites, much less let them enroll, graduate, and eventually teach. The Clarks attended Howard University and then became the first African Americans to receive doctorates from Columbia. They developed a simple method of studying racial bias with even very young children. They would show a child a pair of dolls, one white and the other black, and then ask a series of simple questions: Which doll looks nice? Which doll looks bad? Which doll do you want to play with?

Throughout the 1940s, 1950s, and 1960s, white children showed a consistent tendency to prefer the white dolls. Black children's choices were more varied and shaped by their context. For example, black children in segregated all-black schools preferred the white dolls, suggesting that they were absorbing the same cultural messages of white superiority that the white children were. By the late 1960s, as desegregation was taking place, black children in integrated schools began to show no preference, or sometimes to prefer the black dolls. In the decades since, researchers have run dozens of versions of the doll studies, most focused on children between the ages of three and seven. Among black children, the pattern remains varied and seems tied to their local backgrounds and experiences, as was the case in the original studies. But with white children, the trend is depressingly consistent: They prefer the white dolls today by about the same margin as they did in the 1940s.

The striking finding in the doll studies is that the charting of bias across a period of decades looks a lot more like the regular patterns of discrimination in Devah Pager's field experiments than the changing patterns in surveys. The surveys that reveal little prejudice are the outlier here, which raises the question of to what extent those self-reports can be trusted. When we look at actual behaviors, we see the persistence of bias again and again.

Preferring a doll that looks like you is one thing, but discriminating in a way that harms someone is a far more serious matter. The state of Florida, famous for its transparency due to a set of "sunshine laws," places the mug shot and rap sheet of every inmate in the state prison system online for anyone to see. Psychologist Irene Blair set out to determine whether how long people were sentenced could actually be predicted by their appearance in their mug shots. She showed hundreds of these photos to raters who knew nothing about each individual's offense. The raters judged the inmates on the degree to which they appeared to be African American, from 1 (not at all) to 9 (very much). She then had a legal expert score the seriousness of each inmate's crime, as well as that of any past crimes on his rap sheet. This was not a subjective judgment—the Florida penal code has a ten-point scoring system that specifies the severity of any charge. Providing a false driver's license rates a 1, for example, whereas selling cocaine is a 5 and murder is a 10. These scores were used as statistical controls so that the researchers could measure how different inmates were sentenced for the same crimes.

The researchers found that the "blacker" the inmates looked, the longer they were sentenced for identical offenses. Those near the top of the scale for "blackness" were sentenced between seven and eight months longer than those near the bottom. The features that influenced the raters in assessing blackness must have affected the sentencing judges as well. Interestingly, the effect of looking black applied equally to inmates who were black and those who were white, as listed on their rap sheets. Regardless of their actual race, it was the features that visually communicated blackness that predicted sentencing.

Race seems to bias even the ultimate punishment. In a study using similar methods, psychologist Jennifer Eberhardt examined the imposition of the death sentence in Pennsylvania. In more than six hundred murder cases that were eligible for the death penalty across a period of twenty years, a clear racial disparity emerged: Defendants who looked blacker to independent raters were more likely to be sentenced to death. This only occurred, however, when the murder victim was white. Even if race was never explicitly discussed during deliberations over sentencing, the juries clearly were taking it into account.

The jury box is not the only place where race bias becomes a matter of life or death. For Levar Jones, the trouble started in September 2014 in the parking lot of a Shell station in Columbia, South Carolina. When he stepped out of his white pickup, state trooper Sean Groubert asked, "Can I see your license, please?" Jones, a slim black man in khaki shorts and a polo shirt, had not yet closed the truck door, so he turned around and reached back inside for his wallet. "Get out of the car!" Officer Groubert shouted. "Get out of the car!" By the time the second word "car" was in the air, the sound of gunshots was echoing and the truck window shattered behind Jones.

In the movies, when a gunshot rings out, it makes a bellowing boom, like a cannon. But the officer's handgun made a high-pitched *pop, pop*, and then another *pop, pop*. In the movies, when a man is shot, he looks as if he has been punched by an invisible fist. Mr. Jones looked simply startled. He dropped his wallet, fumbling for a moment to catch it before it fell, and then he returned his attention to the man shooting at him. He jumped and turned his waist to one side, as if an annoying bee had stung him on the hip. Then, realizing what was happening, he raised his hands high in the air and stumbled to the ground, looking incredulously between the wallet on the ground and the man still shooting at him. The episode lasted three seconds.

When the shooting stopped, Jones said, "I just got my license. You said get my license. I grabbed my license." His tone became more urgent: "Right *here*. That's my *license*. *Right there*." He focused intently on the license, the proof of who he was, the proof of his innocence, the proof that could resolve the chaos that was happening. As the police radio chattered about "shots fired," Jones asked, "What did I do, sir? . . . Why did you shoot me? . . . Why were you pulling me over?" Trooper Groubert replied, as calmly as if he'd been asked for the time, "Seat belt violation, sir."

Levar Jones survived that day and recovered from the gunshot wound in his hip. Officer Groubert was fired, and as of this writing has pleaded guilty to charges of aggravated assault and battery.

Killings of unarmed black men by police have become a focal point in America's conversations about race. If you follow the news, you might have an image in your mind of Michael Brown's body lying in a Ferguson, Missouri, street for hours. Or the protests that followed, with lines of riot-geared police illuminated by the fires of burning cars. You might hear Eric Garner's quiet last words, "I can't breathe," as he is asphyxiated by an officer's choke hold. You might mentally replay the grainy images of the video in which a police car pulls up toward fourteen-year-old Tamir Rice, and he crumbles to the ground two seconds later.

At the heart of all these incidents and many more was a subjective perception of what was actually taking place. Was Michael Brown attacking officer Darren Wilson? Was Eric Garner dangerously resisting arrest? Was Tamir Rice drawing a (real) gun? Such judgment calls have to be made under highly stressful conditions. The situation is often ambiguous: The same movement might indicate reaching for a gun or reaching for a driver's license. There is not much time to deliberate such questions. If it's a gun, then taking an extra second of caution could mean the difference between life and death. One of the best-established findings in all of psychology is that people make sense of uncertain or ambiguous circumstances by relying on their expectations. The less time there is to think carefully, the more they depend on them. Watching as incidents with such striking similarities make headlines again and again holds up an unflattering mirror to our culture's expectations of black men.

The cornerstone of legal decision making in cases like these is the "reasonable person test": What would a reasonable person do when faced with such circumstances? But the reasonable person test creates a lot of puzzles when we are dealing with a decision that we know, in retrospect, to have been wrong. Try putting yourself in the position of the police officer encountering Levar Jones. None of us thinks we would make the same mistake. But then again, if Officer Groubert had known it *was* a mistake, he surely wouldn't have made the same choices. The unsettling truth is that we could all make the same kinds of mistakes that the police officers made in these shootings.

In one of the first experiments I conducted as a graduate student, I tested whether the average person was more likely to believe that a harmless object was a dangerous weapon when it was paired with a black person. A police shooting of an unarmed black man named Amadou Diallo had recently made headlines, following an altercation very similar to the one that involved Levar Jones. The police officers claimed that they had sincerely believed that their lives were in danger, even though it turned out that Diallo had only his wallet in his hand. A lot of people were asking themselves what a reasonable person would have done in the officers' situation. Newly armed with the tools of psychology experiments, I set out to find out.

I was just learning how to write the computer code needed to create a computerized game to test the idea, so I tried it out first on myself. For each trial of the game, a photo of a person would flash on the screen, some of whom were black and others who were white. After the photo, an object would flash on the screen. Half of the objects were handguns, and the other half were small tools, like wrenches or pliers. I chose tools because they were similar in color and contours to a gun, were about the same size as one, and were made of metal. After each sequence of person/object was presented, I pressed one key labeled *gun* or another key labeled *tool*. I programmed the game to repeat this sequence—face, object, response; face, object, response—about two hundred times. I completed all two hundred trials, and it felt easy. I checked my data, and I was almost perfectly accurate.

I then added a critical bit of code: The computer now timed how long it took to press the response keys, and if it took longer than half a second, the screen displayed a big red X and the words "Too slow!" I had introduced time pressure into the picture. This transformed the task in an important way. It was no longer a vision test, but one of snap judgments, of split-second decision making, introducing into the laboratory the sort of quick decisions that police officers have to make when a suspect reaches toward his pocket or leans into his car.

I took my test again, and this time it was grueling. I focused my eyes on the exact spot where the pictures appeared. I leaned toward the screen, shoulders hunched in concentration. The harder I tried to beat the big red X, the more mistakes I made. The harder I tried to get it right, the more often I got the big red X. At the end of two hundred repetitions, my neck hurt and I was sweating, not just with exertion, but also out of concern about what my results would reveal. When I looked at my data, I got about 80 percent correct. That was not a bad result, but the pattern of my errors was disturbing: I was much more likely to mistake harmless objects for guns when a black face had been flashed initially.

In a way, these data made no sense. I knew perfectly well that the black faces in this computer game posed no threat. And I knew they were no more likely to be linked to guns than the white faces—I had just written the code myself that assured they were unrelated. I certainly had no reason to be biased, and I was trying my hardest to be accurate.

And yet, in another respect, the data made perfect sense. After all, I was raised in a culture that worries about the kinds of nouns young children will use to describe a black man. I was raised in the same culture as all those landlords and business owners in the field studies, the same culture that Trooper Groubert grew up in.

Sitting there in my lab, trying to beat my own bias test and failing, I felt for the first time the discomforting gap between my good intentions and my biased behavior, known as implicit bias. I felt as if I were that kid in the grocery store all over again. I went on to use that game in dozens of experiments involving thousands of research subjects. Other researchers replicated the findings in their own labs. Again and again I found that same pattern of bias, with people more likely to think they saw a gun when it was linked to a black face. In some versions of the experiment, we even warned the subjects that the race of the face would bias them and urged them to resist that prejudice. But cautioning didn't help, and in fact it made the bias a little worse, because then the topic of race was more prominent in subjects' minds. Good intentions don't defend us against unintended biases.

Shortly after I published my first studies on racially biased threat perceptions, I received a pair of e-mails from readers. One was from a retired police officer who did not appreciate that my research might imply that police officers have that bias. After all, he wrote, they are forced to make life-or-death decisions in a fraction of a second under complex and uncertain conditions. The other letter was from someone describing himself as a civil rights activist. His concern was that by describing the bias we found as unintentional, our research might exonerate police officers rather than holding them responsible for biased actions. With regard to implicit bias, both writers could be right, a dilemma that has challenged psychologists, philosophers, and legal scholars.

Another way to view this dilemma is to reconsider the "reasonable person test." Although not everyone displays bias, the average participant was biased by race. If we assume that the average person is a reasonable person, then we would have to conclude that a reasonable person would indeed be more prone to see danger from an unarmed black man than from an unarmed white man. Logically, then, racial bias is reasonable. That doesn't seem right.

The alternative is to assume that the average person is unreasonable. If we start from that premise, then when a jury decides guilt or innocence by asking what a reasonable person would do, they are demanding a higher standard of the defendant than can be expected of the majority of people. That doesn't seem fair, either. This is the paradox of implicit bias, where actions are uncoupled from intentions, and we don't know where to aim our moral outrage.

Understanding implicit bias requires taking a more nuanced approach to the individuals we are easily tempted to label as "racist" or "not racist." If you consider whether you yourself are biased, and why, you will likely focus on your conscious thoughts and beliefs, your values and good intentions. Having reflected on what a fundamentally good person you are, you will conclude that implicit bias is other people's problem. Although we would all like to believe ourselves to be members of the "not racist" club, we are all steeped in a culture whose history and present is built on massive racial inequality. Research has shown that a majority of even well-meaning people—and their children—show signs of implicit bias when tested.

Here's a quick example of another kind of implicit bias test to try yourself. Read the words below, then complete the word fragment with the first word that comes to mind.

Dog   Scottish   Jack   Russell   Ter_____.

Now read this second set of words and complete the word fragment with the first word that comes to mind.

Mohammed   Mosque   Islamic   Ter_____.

I bet your thought was "terrier" for the first blank and "terrorist" for the second one. To make that prediction I don't need to know anything about your beliefs and values. I don't need to know your politics. All I need to know is that you are immersed in a culture that links Islam with terrorism in its web of associations. As a result, your brain makes those links, too.

The human mind is often compared to a computer, but it's more like the Internet itself: a dense web of interconnections of ideas and information. Like the Internet, that web of associations contains plenty of smut and nonsense along with indispensable knowledge. Implicit biases are the raw, uncensored results of traveling along those associative links. And, as with the Internet, sometimes what is on the other end of a link is disturbing.

Studies suggest that implicit bias is much more prevalent today than old-fashioned bigotry. Although implicit bias is widespread, recent research suggests that people are more biased in some situations than others, and that the differences are linked to money, power, and inequality. That economic status and prejudice are interrelated is itself an old concept. For example, a study published in 1940 found that when the price of cotton fell in the South, the number of black people lynched by white mobs increased. When economic hardship plagued white farmers, the authors argued, they took their frustration out on black people. A few decades of squabbling about the statistical methods of this study ensued, but modern analyses using more sophisticated statistics have upheld the original work's conclusion: Economic anxieties fuel racial conflict.

Today links between economic status and racial bias still exist, albeit in much more subtle forms. In one study, psychologists Amy Krosch and David Amodio gave white study subjects ten dollars with which to play an economic game. They made some subjects feel disadvantaged by saying that they could have received up to a hundred dollars, but—sorry—they got only ten. A comparison group was told that they had received ten out of ten possible dollars, so that they did not feel as if they had lost out. Both groups were then asked to classify a set of photos of biracial people as either black or white. Subjects in the relatively poor condition perceived the biracial images as having darker skin and looking more stereotypically black than those in the relatively rich condition. Feeling disadvantaged magnified their perception of racial differences, increasing the distance between whom these white subjects saw as "us" and "them."

Other research has shown that occupying a superior position also increases implicit bias. One study, for example, assigned subjects to be either "bosses" or "workers." They worked in pairs on a problem-solving task, and the boss gave orders to the worker, then evaluated the worker's results afterward. Subjects who were in the role of bosses showed greater implicit racial bias than those assigned to be workers, or than those in a control group that didn't participate in the problem-solving interaction at all.

These studies suggest that being either disadvantaged or advantaged can increase racial bias. Aren't those two findings contradictory? Not really. Imagine two companies that have a racially diverse group of employees. Company A is laid-back and not very hierarchical—imagine a tech start-up in Silicon Valley, with Ping-Pong tables and a beer garden and scooters to ride around the office. Yes, there is a boss, but she wears jeans and sits at the communal desks while working on her iPad, like everyone else. There's not really a chain of command. People work in loosely affiliated problem-based teams, and when they move from one project to another, the teams dissolve.

Company B is more traditional and hierarchical. There is a strict chain of command in which the senior executive sits in the corner office and gives orders to middle management, who passes the buck down the hierarchy. If employees have a problem, going "over the boss's head" is unthinkable.

Which company do you think is going to have more harmonious relationships across racial lines? The hierarchy of the second company sets up conditions for bias and conflict. When everyone is either a superior or a subordinate, the hierarchy constantly highlights differences in status. The effects of hierarchies extend beyond small-scale organizations like companies. We saw in earlier chapters that nations and states with higher income inequality place a higher emphasis on status and hierarchy, so it stands to reason that they would also have higher levels of race bias. In support of that argument, an analysis of police shootings across the country found that unarmed black men were three and a half times more likely to be shot than unarmed whites overall. But the disparity was higher in counties with higher income inequality.

Not only does income inequality heighten racial bias, but prejudice can also perpetuate income inequality. Decades of studies have found a strong correlation between dislike of black people and opposition to social welfare policies aimed at helping the poor. For example, political scientist Martin Gilens found that most Americans believe inequality is too high, and seven in ten think that government spending to help the poor should be increased. And yet, by the same margin, Americans think welfare spending should be cut. "Welfare" simply refers to the suite of race-neutral government programs aimed at helping the poor, so these results don't make much sense on their surface.

But it turns out that when Americans talk about "the poor," they mean something very different from when they talk about "welfare recipients." The best predictor of wanting to slash funding for welfare recipients is racial prejudice. People who believe that black Americans are lazy and undeserving are the most likely to oppose welfare spending.

Racial bias is not the only reason that people could be against welfare spending, of course. Economists have pointed out that middle- and upper-class citizens have a rational interest in opposing welfare spending. From their perspective, cutting taxes on the affluent and cutting benefits to the poor is simply the self-interested thing to do. People might similarly oppose welfare spending on principled ideological grounds. They might value hard work and self-reliance, and as such regard welfare as a dependency trap, a position often taken by politicians and political elites. But Gilens's studies find no evidence that these are major motivations for ordinary citizens. Statistically speaking, if you want to predict who is predisposed against welfare, you can mostly ignore their economic principles. What you really need to know is their prejudices.

While it may not be surprising that the average person views welfare in racially tinged terms, the truth is that welfare recipients are about evenly divided among white, black, and Hispanic recipients. But when Gilens analyzed depictions of welfare recipients in television and newsmagazines since the 1960s, he found a clear racial bias: When welfare recipients were depicted as the "deserving poor," they were mostly white, but when they were portrayed as lazy and dishonest, they were overwhelmingly black.

This cultural messaging linking welfare to lazy people in general and lazy black people in particular makes it difficult to discuss welfare without racial overtones. This association fuels debates about "dog-whistle politics," in which many people hear coded messages about race in what are ostensibly straightforward policy statements. Ronald Reagan's famous comments about "welfare queens" driving Cadillacs outraged Democrats, though Reagan denied his remark had anything to do with race. His case was not helped when his adviser Lee Atwater described coded racial messages as a central component of the Republican "Southern strategy" in a 1981 interview: "By 1968 you can't say 'ni**er'—that hurts you. Backfires. So you say stuff like forced busing, states' rights and all that stuff. You're getting so abstract now you're talking about cutting taxes, and all these things you're talking about are totally economic things and a byproduct of them is blacks get hurt worse than whites. And subconsciously maybe that's part of it."

More recently, House Speaker Paul Ryan was accused of dog-whistling when he explained poverty as a "tailspin of culture, in our inner cities in particular, of men not working and just generations of men not even thinking about working. . . ." He, too, later claimed that his comment had nothing to do with race.

We can't know for certain what the intent of these leaders was. Did they mean to stir up racial divisions in the minds of white voters while maintaining plausible deniability? Or did they genuinely seek to be racially neutral while members of the opposing party interpreted their comments cynically? The fact is, if you support Reagan and Ryan, you will be inclined to give them the benefit of the doubt. But if you distrust them, you are more likely to view them as making none-too-subtle racially tinged comments.

The interesting observation from a psychological point of view is that the intention of the speaker ultimately doesn't matter. What does matter is how the audience interprets his words. The notion of racially coded messaging—intentional or not—assumes a psychological leap on the part of listeners. It assumes that when politicians talk about policies, voters naturally connect them to race. My collaborators Jazmin Brown-Iannuzzi, Erin Cooley, Ron Dotsch, and I recently tested whether people really make this psychological leap. We wanted to determine whether, when citizens are asked about welfare recipients, their mind's eye viewed them as black people.

To find that out, we needed a way to visualize our subjects' mental representations. We began by creating a composite photo consisting of selected facial features from a black man, a black woman, a white man, and a white woman. To this androgynous biracial face, we added random visual noise, like static on a TV screen. We repeated this exercise hundreds of times until we had a large set of faces where each looked slightly different and slightly blurry. We then showed research participants pairs from this group of photos and asked them to select which one looked more like a welfare recipient. By morphing together all of the images that had been judged to be the "welfare recipient" and then morphing those that had been chosen as the "non–welfare recipient," we then created two new composite photos.

The images that emerged captured subjects' images of what a welfare recipient looked like. When we showed pairs of unlabeled images to a new set of participants, they described the welfare recipient image as a black man and the image of the non-recipient as a white man. They judged the welfare recipient as looking lazy,

Figure 7.2. Mental images of the typical welfare recipient (left) and non-recipient (right).

irresponsible, hostile, and unintelligent. Chillingly, they also regarded the welfare recipient as being less human. You can see clearly defined eyes in the image of the non-recipient, but the eyes of the welfare recipient are hollow.

Next, we tested whether these mental images actually cause differences in support for welfare benefits. We showed the images of the typical welfare recipient and the non-recipient, without identifying them, to another group of subjects and asked whether they would be in favor of providing food stamps and cash assistance to each. When they imagined giving benefits to the non-recipient, they were generally supportive. But when they pictured giving benefits to the welfare recipient, they were opposed. The very qualities that people envision about welfare recipients are the qualities that lead them to oppose giving them benefits.

We have seen in this chapter how tightly race and inequality are intertwined. Economic inequality creates a status-based us-and-them mentality that heightens race bias. And the close connections between race, poverty, and deservingness in the minds of citizens are a major obstacle to reducing economic inequality. Many people simply don't feel very motivated to support fighting poverty when they imagine that minorities will be the beneficiaries.

Acknowledging the existence of racial bias makes many citizens feel hopeless, because it seems so hard to change. Implicit bias seems especially difficult, because it resides not just in the minds of individuals but in the nebulous current of people and ideas that make up the culture around us. Recent research, however, raises some grounds for optimism. Millions of people have taken an implicit bias test at projectimplicit.com, a website where you can test yourself for biases related to race, gender, age, and other social groups. Psychologist Dominic Packer investigated which American states showed the highest and lowest levels of race bias, and what elements distinguished them.

One of the most important factors was income inequality. States with lower inequality had less implicit bias, even after accounting for average income and regional differences between the North and South. Low-inequality states like Oregon, Washington, and Vermont had much less bias than high-inequality Louisiana, New Jersey, or Pennsylvania. Although it may be difficult to change people's hearts and minds, economic policies can certainly reduce income inequality.

We have seen in previous chapters how the social comparisons we make can alter how we see the world. That also holds true for how we understand racial inequality. The gulf between the views of white and black citizens about current levels of prejudice reflects not only different daily experiences, but also different kinds of comparisons, according to research led by psychologist Richard Eibach. If you ask white respondents how well the country is doing in overcoming racism, they look to the past as a frame of reference. Compared with the bad old days of slavery and Jim Crow, we seem to be making good progress, they will assert. But if you ask black respondents the same question, they look to the future: Compared with what life would be like in a country with true equality, the current situation looks fairly bleak.

White and black people don't inhabit completely different worlds, however. The researchers found that if you invite black and white participants to make the kinds of comparisons the other group tends to make, they end up agreeing. If you urge blacks to think about how bad their status was in the past, then their assessments of the present become more optimistic. And if you encourage whites to imagine what a future with true equality would look like, they become less satisfied and more motivated to change the status quo. Consider this chapter an invitation to look forward.

Chapter 8

The Corporate Ladder
Why Fair Pay Signals Fair Play

Elmer Ruiz dug graves for a living. He lived with his wife and children on the grounds of a Chicago cemetery. The grassy burial grounds were the children's playground, except when there was an interment, when they had to stay indoors. After digging graves each day, Ruiz attended each burial to make sure things went smoothly. "There are some funerals, they really affect you," he said. "Some young kid. We buried lots of young." To hide his emotions during the ceremonies, he said, "I usually will wear myself some black sunglasses."

People constantly asked Ruiz, "How can you take it?" You might be surprised at his answer. "I enjoy it very much," he explained. "Especially in the summer. I don't think any job inside a factory or an office is so nice. You have the air all day, and it's just beautiful."

Surely, you might object, Ruiz can't be serious—he can't possibly enjoy digging graves for a living. But his response is not unusual. Researchers have found that people who do "dirty work"—the gravediggers, coal miners, and slaughterhouse workers of the world—tend to have a surprisingly positive view of their jobs. It's not that they all love what they do, but rather that they don't love it much less than people with supposedly "good jobs" enjoy their own work. One recent survey, for example, found that

95 percent of physicians were satisfied with their jobs, and as such constitute the most satisfied category. But it also found that 85 percent of bus drivers—the least satisfied category—were also satisfied with their careers. The key for most workers is not *what* they are doing, but what it *means* to them. What work means to people often has less to do with what tasks they are actually performing than with how they relate to and compare themselves to other people.

While Elmer Ruiz felt bad for the poor wretches working in office jobs, they would likely pity him. When I published my first scientific article, I proudly enclosed a copy of it in a letter I sent to my brother, who, as I mentioned earlier, was in prison at the time. He wrote back that he really appreciated receiving the package. He had recently begun feeling depressed about being stuck there, working for pennies per hour, he explained, until he saw what I did all day. Our relationship with our work, like so many parts of life, is relative.

The curious relationship between people and their work was discovered, in large part, by the United States Army during World War II. When the bombing of Pearl Harbor launched the country into the conflict, the army ballooned from a quarter million men to a million and a half within one year. Increasing the size of the army by a factor of five so quickly created a number of problems, both logistical and human. In the soft light of nostalgia, we remember the "Greatest Generation" today for their bravery and stoicism. But things did not look so rosy from inside the army at the time.

Many of the new soldiers were draftees who lacked the discipline of regular soldiers. Officers complained that the new recruits slouched, did not salute, questioned orders, and complained constantly. They even bucked the chain of command—unheard of in the army—and wrote letters complaining to generals and Congress members. The collision of a million men accustomed to being free citizens and a military chain of command accustomed to unquestioning obedience caused an epidemic of what the officers called "low morale."

Into this crisis stepped Samuel Stouffer, a sociology professor who was tapped to lead the army's research branch. Stouffer used survey research and statistical analysis—cutting-edge techniques at the time—to try to understand what motivated soldiers. In finding after finding, his research challenged the officers' conventional wisdom. For example, he found that hatred of the enemy was much less important in motivating soldiers than the officers had thought. Much more important was the desire to not let down their fellow troops. Stouffer also discovered that actual combat experience surprisingly decreased hatred of the enemy rather than increasing it. Soldiers who had never left America hated the Germans and the Japanese with greater intensity than those in the battlefield. The forces fighting the Germans hated the Japanese more than they hated the Germans, while those fighting the Japanese reserved their worst hatred for the Germans. Contradicting the officers' assumption that combat bred hatred and hatred fueled combat, Stouffer found that it was easier to hate from a safe distance than from within the intimate terror of battle.

When Stouffer turned his attention to what made soldiers like or dislike their jobs, he again found evidence that seemed to defy common sense. He discovered that military policemen, who had little chance for advancement, were more satisfied with their prospects than air corpsmen, who enjoyed rapid promotions. He also learned that black soldiers had higher morale in the South than black soldiers in the North, even though it seemed that they were treated much better in the North. These early observations were not a fluke. When Stouffer looked systematically across the branches of the army, soldiers were more satisfied in divisions with the least room for moving up the ranks. Why would people be happier in such situations?

The answer, Stouffer realized, was that soldiers compared themselves to others who were in positions like their own: Military policemen compared themselves to other policemen, and air corpsmen compared themselves to other corpsmen. In the relatively flat hierarchy of the military police, no rank differed too significantly from any other. But in the much more hierarchical air corps, the fact that some soldiers were dramatically higher in rank than others bred resentment in the average soldier. Thus the idea of "relative deprivation" was born. Stouffer's research was the first in a long tradition of studies finding that relative standing in a hierarchy matters as much as or more than tangible rewards associated with a particular rank.

The workplace is where most people experience inequality most directly on a daily basis. In this chapter we explore how equality and inequality in pay, status, and power shape the meaning we assign to our work.

Workplaces are organized as hierarchies, in part because just about everything humans do is arranged in that structure. In one classic study, groups of strangers were brought together for a one-hour discussion session and given little direction about what to do otherwise. Without any instructions from the researchers, these groups sorted themselves into hierarchies with leaders directing the discussion and subordinates following. If you observe people gathering together, whether in backyard barbecues or hanging out on a street corner or in a college classroom, they tend to organize themselves into little hierarchies. The more dominant "leaders" take up more physical space, talk more, and have more influence on group interactions, while the more deferential followers toe the line.

If even everyday situations give rise to hierarchies, it's not surprising that workplaces are even more prone to do so. In fact, when scholars have tried to study organizations that function without one, they can't seem to find any. For example, the design firm IDEO is famous for its lack of a hierarchical structure. When it was founded in the 1990s, it had the look and feel of a Silicon Valley start-up. Almost all of its employees had the same title: engineer. Although it lacked a formal hierarchy, when scholars observed the daily routines of its employees, they saw status differences everywhere. The engineers competed during brainstorming sessions to develop creative ideas, and those who had a reputation for coming up with the best ones received more deference from others, and were paid more. Those who had contributed less stopped getting invitations to the brainstorming sessions and would eventually leave the company. Such gradations in status, influence, and pay are the heart of any hierarchy. Some companies are just more up front about it than others.

In some ways, hierarchies can help an organization function better. The ability to move up the company ladder might provide an incentive to work harder. Another advantage is that hierarchies provide clear rules about the roles and expectations of people in various positions, which can reduce conflict and help each person define his or her job. Most important, hierarchies enable people to specialize in the areas in which they are most skilled. Executives in a pharmaceutical company, for example, need to know how to manage an organization, but they don't have to know how to do bench chemistry. The chemists, meanwhile, don't need to worry about market strategies.

Given all the ways that hierarchy can be beneficial, you'd think that it would be good for business, and that the more hierarchy in a company, the better. Alas, it's not that simple. A hierarchy can be organized well or poorly. Increasingly, it seems it is done poorly. To understand why that might be the case, consider this question: Who do you think has a more stressful job—the corporate executive or the office worker inhabiting the cube farm outside the corner office?

Many believe that it is the hard-charging, type-A, coronary-prone executive, thumbing e-mails on his smartphone when he should be at his kid's Little League practice. A recent *Wall Street Journal* article described the plight of one CEO who had to drag himself out of bed each morning and muster his game face before facing a long day of telling other people what to do. The situation became so bad, we are told, that he had no choice but to take a year off from his job to sail across the Atlantic Ocean with his family.

Forbes agrees: "Many CEOs have personal assistants who run their schedules for them, and they go from one meeting straight to another with barely a moment to go to the bathroom." The indignity! And even worse than the bladder strain is the pressure of having to fire people: "You may think a CEO can be detached when deciding who to lay off, but generally that couldn't be farther from the truth. Having to make tough decisions about the people all around you can hit very hard."

Firing people certainly sounds stressful, although not quite as bad as, well, actually being fired. In fact, the empirical data turn the above examples on their heads. A study by psychologist Gary Sherman and colleagues provides the most direct evidence yet of the difference in stress experienced by leaders and followers. They assessed full-time workers in either business or the military who were taking executive education classes at Harvard's business school. The participants were classified as either leaders or nonleaders, with leaders defined as those whose job required them to manage other people. On both surveys of anxiety and biological measures of the stress hormone cortisol, the people taking direction showed substantially higher levels of stress than those giving the directions. The results were the same in both the business and military subjects.

One of the reasons that hierarchy is stressful for people at the bottom is that they often lack control over how and when they do their work. I experienced the importance of control as I made my way through a series of jobs in college. Each seemed better than the last. My first job was waiting tables at a Ponderosa Steakhouse. The tips were about a dollar per table, and tax on them was withheld from the wage, which meant I was working entirely for the tips. Because the tips were so low, we handled six to ten tables at a time.

My favorite thing about waiting tables was that the time flew by. From the moment I clocked in, I would be juggling the drink orders from one table, delivering the food to another, and clearing away the dirty dishes from another, while noticing out of the corner of my eye that two more tables had just been seated in my section. The six-hour shift would pass in a blur, and at the end of it my feet would hurt but I didn't feel tired; my heart was still racing and the adrenaline and cortisol were still pumping through my veins.

Being interested in psychology, I then eagerly took a job at a place called a mental health "crisis stabilization unit." The concept behind this establishment was that the state could save a lot of money if it could avoid committing mentally ill people, most of whom were indigent, to a state hospital. It rented a house for them, and rather than employing expensive doctors, the place was staffed with a nurse, some recent college graduates, and a group of college students. Patients would come in, often hallucinating, suicidal, or both. We would watch them and try our best to keep them from doing anything to harm themselves until they could get an outpatient appointment with a psychiatrist to prescribe medications. The first night was always tense, as you waited to see whether the main problem was drugs (in which case the hallucinations would wear off) or a psychotic disorder (in which case they wouldn't).

Each overnight shift had one full-time college graduate and one part-time student on staff. There were many nights when the full-time staffer had to leave to pick up a new patient, leaving the student to tend to several unmedicated psychiatric patients and

every suicidal person with a phone in Warren County. In retrospect, it was an awful lot of responsibility for a twenty-year-old
whose main qualification was that he thought psychology was
neat. I received some minimal training about what to do when a
suicidal person called for help, but all I can remember is that I felt
it was important to "keep them talking" so they didn't do anything rash.

The curious thing is, that job was much less nerve-racking
than waiting tables. Certainly, the stakes were higher, but the
psychiatric patients were seldom very demanding. If you have
never worked in a service job, it may be hard to understand how
six people demanding Dr Pepper refills can be more anxiety-
provoking than one person having an existential crisis. And yet
being asked to do more than you can do simultaneously is inher-
ently anxiety-provoking. It's like concentrating all your attention
on trying to remember a phone number while someone is shout-
ing numbers nearby. Everything a waiter does involves time pressure, and she can never just say, "I'm busy—I'll get back to you."

The crisis stabilization unit was an improvement over waiting
tables, but both paled in comparison to the amount of control I experienced working for an answering service. I'm not sure if answering services still exist, given the current prevalence of automated
phone menus, but if they do, you would probably never realize that
you had actually encountered one, because an answering service is
essentially a telephonic cloaking device.

The employees would sit in a room full of cubicles wearing
microphone headsets and answer the phones for dozens of businesses in town. We could never let the caller know he had reached
a service rather than the business itself but had to create the illusion that if he phoned Billy's Plumbing at three in the morning, it
was Billy's highly trained team of receptionists that was waiting
to take his call. That scenario could all go wrong if callers started
asking reasonable questions, like, "Is Billy there or isn't he?" It

was then that we relied on our advanced training in the Orwellian art of "call control." Call control is the skill, practiced by answering service operators and politicians the world over, of suppressing the natural human inclination to answer a question that another human has asked you. Our mission was to get a name, a phone number, and a one-line description of the nature of the call, and then get off the phone as quickly as possible.

Although I was not rising in any hierarchy—I was on the bottom rung in every position—the reason that each of these successive jobs (even the answering service one) felt increasingly satisfying was that I gained more and more control over my own work and my interactions with my colleagues. Ordinarily, increased control goes hand in hand with higher rank and pay. But the ways that pay inequality affects productivity and job satisfaction are complex and often surprising. Inequalities in pay are supposed to be motivational. If more productive workers are rewarded for their labors, the theory goes, then everyone will work harder to achieve higher wages. This kind of pay-for-performance makes perfect economic sense. Unfortunately, people are not very good at obeying the laws of economics. Pay inequalities might drive motivation, but they can also drive resentments.

If you are a manager and you want to use pay differentials to motivate your employees, then you would ideally want to be transparent about how much each worker receives. Only if the staff has full information about how much people earn at each level in the organization can they adjust their striving accordingly. In practice, however, most companies have formal policies or informal norms preventing this information from becoming public. Pay secrecy makes sense only if you believe that the effects of pay inequality on resentment will trump its effects on performance.

Pay secrecy also sets the stage for trouble when someone can't keep a secret. Just such a secret was leaked by mischievous researchers in one study of how pay inequality affects workers. In 2008 the *Sacramento Bee* launched a website listing the salary of every California state employee. These included the entire work-force of the University of California system. A team of researchers led by economist David Card had the idea to inform some of the university faculty and staff about the website and see how it af-fected their job satisfaction. They sent thousands of employees in one group an e-mail alerting them to the website and providing a helpful link so they could easily look up salaries themselves. An-other group served as the control, and was not sent the e-mail. A few days later both groups were sent a survey about their job sat-isfaction and how likely they were to change jobs in the upcom-ing year.

Not surprisingly, hits to the salary website spiked. Learning about their colleagues' pay had a big effect on the employees' hap-piness with their own jobs, but it depended on how much money they made. For those who earned less than the average in their department, this knowledge made them much less satisfied and more interested in looking elsewhere for work. But for those who were paid above average, the revelation of their superior income did not make them feel highly satisfied. In fact, it had virtually no effect.

Three years after the survey, the researchers followed up with the subjects who had been sent the salary website to see who had moved on from their jobs. The workers paid less than average were now much less likely to be currently employed by the uni-versity. It wasn't simply the low salary that had motivated them to depart, because the lower-paid workers in the control group did not leave at such high rates. Instead, it was the awareness that they were paid less than their coworkers that mattered.

The University of California study found that high levels of pay inequality reduced the satisfaction of those at the bottom with-out increasing the happiness of those at the top, which challenges the pay-for-performance theory. But that research did not investigate job performance. Could pay inequality still have motivated higher performance? Productivity and performance are hard to measure in a university setting because "productive" has very different meanings when applied to researchers, teachers, and administrators. Other studies have addressed the performance question in an arena where the metric could not be clearer: major league sports.

In one study, economist Matt Bloom tallied the wins and losses of every Major League Baseball team over an eight-year period. In keeping with the theory that pay inequality motivates better performance, you would predict that the teams with greater pay differentials would win more games. In baseball, like the American economy, higher inequality is almost entirely driven by the extremely lucrative salaries of the best-paid players. Did granting their stars enormous salaries increase a team's wins?

Bloom found exactly the opposite to be the case. The teams with the greatest levels of pay inequality performed worse than those with less inequality. Similar effects were found in an NFL study: Football teams with greater inequality won fewer games. This research also revealed an interesting wrinkle: Higher pay inequality was associated with *higher* team revenues. The most likely explanation for this finding is that spending huge amounts of money to attract superstars increases fans' willingness to pay for tickets and media to watch these celebrity players, even if their expensive contracts undermined the team's overall performance.

But why might pay inequality undermine performance? Its major downside is that it can create resentment and therefore weaken cooperation and teamwork. To test this argument, we need to look beyond just the number of wins and losses to investigate in greater detail the performance of individual players.

Researchers love baseball, because copious statistics are recorded about players' performances in every game. Bloom looked up the statistics for all 1,644 players in the leagues during the same period as his original study. Not surprisingly, the highly paid players performed better than their lower-paid teammates. But his striking finding was that the superstars on high-inequality teams performed worse than the superstars on low-inequality teams. If pay inequality served to motivate the performance of the stars, you would expect just the opposite result. Higher inequality seemed to undercut the superstar players it was meant to incentivize, which is what you would expect if you believed that the chief effect of pay inequality was to reduce cooperation and team cohesion. As in the University of California study, the harmful effects of inequality on morale and teamwork outweighed the positive effects on performance.

Pay inequality does not always undercut performance, though. In studies of professional golf, tournaments with greater inequality in the winners' purses are linked to better golfing scores. Likewise, a study of NASCAR racing revealed that greater inequality in the prize money led to faster racing. There is a critical difference between performance in a team sport, like baseball or football, and that in individual sports, like golf and racing. In the latter, a single contestant can focus harder or change his strategy when there is more money on the line. But in team sports, a group's ability to work together outweighs the talent of any one member. For that reason, the disruptive effect of inequality on team coordination can outweigh the motivating effect on particular individuals.

In understanding the effects of inequality at work, we have to consider whether the workplace functions more like a team sport or like a solo sport. Some jobs are essentially solo sports. If you are a truck driver whose responsibility consists of driving alone for hours or days at a time, then a bigger gap between the best-paid and worst-paid truckers in your company may motivate better performance in the form of, say, longer hours. But the vast majority of workplaces in the modern economy require teamwork. Even relatively solitary jobs like computer programming usually require becoming part of a team to accomplish a larger project at least some of the time.

The tendency for inequality to compromise team performance is not limited to sports. One massive study of dozens of corporations compared the quality of the products the companies produced, as rated by independent executives who were experts in each product area. They found that the greater the pay inequality between executives versus hourly workers, the lower the quality of what they produced. Most products are the outcome of a long and complex production chain involving thousands of interactions among workers at all different levels in the firm. The more teamlike a workplace is, the more likely it is that the harmful effects of resentment over inequality will negate the motivating effects of incentives.

What employees want is not equality, exactly. They understand that someone with advanced training, skills, and experience will be paid more than an unskilled novice worker. What people desire is a fair balance between what they contribute and how they are rewarded. Think of it as a ratio, the simplest expression of which is dollars per hour worked. There are other kinds of rewards besides money, however, and other kinds of contributions besides the amount of work done.

When that ratio of reward to contribution is out of balance, people try to restore it. The interesting thing about this particular formula is that it can be made more favorable either by increasing the rewards or by reducing the contribution. In the simple case of pay per hour, that means either raising wages (for the same amount of work done) or reducing the hours worked (for the same level of pay). When employees feel they are not being compensated appropriately for their work, they can negotiate for more pay and benefits, but when that doesn't work or is simply not possible, they can often become more creative in their methods.

They can slack off, like Adam, a university maintenance worker interviewed by author Martin Sprouse. Adam described how he would regularly drive his maintenance truck to a coworker's house during the work day and take a nap.

Another way to improve the balance is to increase pay by stealing, like Roy, a shipping clerk at a liquor warehouse. The company was moving from Boston to Louisville and was planning to lay off all its employees. On the final day, he was supposed to load up the remaining bottles and send them to Kentucky. But resenting the company's lack of loyalty to its employees, Roy delivered those last 200 cases to the houses of his warehouse coworkers instead, giving them their own version of a severance package.

Sometimes restoring the balance takes more insidious forms, as with P.J.K., a stockbroker. One day he realized he could execute large trades by using a shared phone on the trading floor, which could not be traced back to him. So he would pick up the phone, dial numbers randomly to carry out nonsensical trades, and then run to a computer screen to watch the chaos he had caused in the markets.

While stealing profits the thief at least, outright sabotage can lead to senseless damage. Sprouse's subjects include a postal employee who destroyed entire bins of mail and a pineapple packer who would send gloves through the slicing machine in order to break it. The most diabolical saboteur was an auto factory worker who put BBs in carburetors so that they would roll around and cause cars to break down intermittently in ways that would seem maddeningly random. These acts seem senseless, until we remember the balance that people are trying to achieve. Altering the ratio of rewards to contributions by making such *negative* contributions won't improve a bank account, but it can balance accounts emotionally. When Adam, the university maintenance worker, was asked why he slacked off on the job, he said he did not think of it as revenge, but as a fair give and take. From Adam's point of view, his ratio of reward and contribution had been restored to a better balance by contributing less.

When researchers coded the motives for bad behavior among workers in hundreds of Sprouse's interviews, they found that the most common were a sense of injustice and a lack of control. While such accounts are only anecdotal, another study looked more systematically at how injustice motivates bad behavior at work. The researchers partnered with an auto parts manufacturing firm that operated three factories. The company had recently lost its contracts with a major customer and was going to have to temporarily cut its workers' pay until it could make up the lost revenue. The researchers persuaded the company to turn the painful pay cuts into a real-life experiment.

At one of its factories, the management told the employees about the lost contracts and informed them that they would be docked a 15 percent pay cut for the next ten weeks. At a second factory, it spared the employees any pay cut. The researchers then worked with the company's accountants to measure how much "shrinkage" there was in the factories' inventories. In other words, they took account of how much of the factories' merchandise and equipment mysteriously disappeared.

In the ten weeks leading up to the pay cuts, both factories had the same rates of shrinkage—less than 3 percent of the factory goods had vanished. But during the ten weeks of reduced pay, the factory that suffered the pay cuts saw its shrinkage triple. To confirm that the effects they saw were actually motivated by the pay cuts, the researchers continued monitoring shrinkage during the ten weeks after regular pay levels had been restored. Theft rates returned back to the precut levels.

Were the employees stealing because they needed more money to get by? Or was it a sense of injustice that inspired the theft as a means to even the score? I mentioned earlier that there was a third factory, which the researchers used to shed light on why thefts had increased. In this facility, management also cut pay by 15 percent, but rather than bluntly announcing the measure, it offered the context and the reasoning for the cut, explaining that it could avoid laying anyone off only by reducing everyone's pay. The plant's manager emphasized that he and the entire management team would be taking the same pay cut as everyone else. In this factory, the theft rate rose only slightly during the pay cut, remaining under 5 percent. The theft, as these results suggested, was mainly a matter of adjusting a ratio of rewards to contributions when the workers saw it as unfair.

We have seen that when workers experience a loss of control, they become stressed, and when they sense they are being treated unfairly, they get even. While cutting pay is one surefire way to generate a feeling of injustice, there are many others. As we have seen, people judge their own pay by comparing it to other people's, which suggests that the stagnant wages of ordinary workers paired with ever rising executive pay in recent years is giving rise to an especially ominous trend.

The study of University of California employees demonstrated that workers can be dissatisfied about inequality only when they are cognizant of it. Recent research in both the United States and globally has indicated that people are unaware of just how unequal most corporations are. One study, which surveyed citizens from forty countries around the world, asked respondents to estimate how much the average unskilled worker was paid per year in their country and how much the average chairperson of a large company made. They then asked how much the average worker and the average chief executive *should* ideally earn. The researchers then computed the ratio of CEO pay to the average worker's pay.

In every country, people's ideal degree of inequality was less than their estimates of actual inequality. On average, respondents thought that CEOs made 10 times as much as the average worker. Their ideal scenario, in contrast, was that CEOs would average 4.6 times as much. One of the striking aspects of these findings is the degree of consensus. People who described themselves as politically left of center thought that CEOs should make 4 times as much as average workers, while those who identified themselves as right of center thought the ideal would be 5 times. Respondents in the lowest 20 percent of the income bracket thought that CEOs should make 4.3 times as much as average workers, while those in the richest 20 percent thought it should be 5 times. People's ideals were surprisingly uniform across age, education levels, and every variable the researchers examined.

The striking global consensus about how much pay inequality people would accept was exceeded only by the astonishing global ignorance about how much inequality actually exists. In every country tested, respondents dramatically underestimated the degree of actual pay inequity. In the United States, for example, people estimated that CEOs earned about 30 times the average worker. In reality, the researchers point out, the average CEO earned $12.3 million in 2012. That is about 350 times the average worker's income of $35,000.

Americans think that CEOs make about a million dollars per year. If we plotted this amount on the human-sized income distribution figure from the introductory chapter, it would be just above the elbows. Plotting the true value of $12 million, however, would require eight men standing on one another's heads. Workers don't expect CEOs to earn $35,000 any more than they expect to earn $12 million themselves. But the ratio of 350 to 1 is enough to insult the sense of fairness of most of them. While a top executive is worth more to a company than the average worker, is he or she worth 350 times more?

It is hard to quantify the exact value of a CEO, but studies have been able to make rough estimates. By examining the performance of many corporations over the course of years, researchers can identify how much of a firm's fortunes are linked to who is at its helm. It seems reasonable to assume that some CEOs are better than others, and that the companies headed by the best of them should earn more money. But there are many other factors that contribute to earnings that CEOs can't control. So how much effect does a top executive really have on a company's success?

In one comprehensive analysis of thousands of corporations over nearly two decades, management professor Markus Fitza found that only about 5 percent of the performance differences between companies could be attributed to the CEO. Other factors played a much larger role. Fluctuations in the economy affect businesses in ways that a CEO can't do anything about. Some industries, like banking, are more profitable than others, like farming. Some companies were more successful than others before the current CEO ever took charge. Fitza estimates than in addition to these uncontrollable elements, about 70 percent of a company's performance, for which the CEO normally gets credit and blame, is a matter of pure random chance. When a corporation sets out to find a new chief executive, it often hires headhunters and consulting firms, spending months of work and millions of dollars to pick just the right candidate. Fitza's research suggests that they might as well have identified a pool of applicants with the general qualifications required for the job, and then just pulled names out of a hat.

People tend to resist accepting that outcomes they care about are due to chance. Studies have shown repeatedly that professional stock investors cannot consistently beat an index fund that reflects the entire market. Die-hard soda drinkers cannot reliably distinguish Coke from Pepsi in a blind taste test. And blindfolded professional violinists cannot tell whether they are playing a Stradivarius or an ordinary violin. And yet how much time and effort are devoted to picking stocks, buying brand-name sodas, and saving a lifetime for the chance at that $3 million Strad?

Not surprisingly the results of Fitza's analysis have been controversial. Others have reanalyzed the data using different statistical techniques and found that the CEO effect might be as high as 22 percent. Other estimates fall somewhere in the middle. Regardless of whether the true number turns out closer to 5 percent or 22 percent, it will be hard to convince workers that the CEO is worth his salary.

The extreme inequality seen today in CEO pay is likely to undermine job satisfaction, team performance, and product quality. It may inspire workers to slack off, steal, and sabotage. These tendencies have probably been kept in check, so far, by the general lack of awareness of how unequal the pay scales really are. But as CEO remuneration reaches new heights, it is becoming more and more often a matter of public knowledge.

In 2015 corporations were required for the first time to publicly disclose the ratio of CEO pay to that of the average employee. It is too early to know if this public dissemination of information will have any effect on workers' morale. But it is clear that awareness of pay inequality is beginning to increase. Three fourths of Americans already believe that CEO pay is too high, and nearly two thirds believe that it should be capped. Imagine what might happen once they learn the truth.

Chapter 9

The Art of Living Vertically

Flatter Ladders, Comparing with Care,
and the Things That Matter Most

The studies in this book each examine one aspect of inequality. To make scientific progress, it is necessary to divide a complex problem into simpler parts and understand how each one works. But the pieces eventually have to be assembled into a whole, as real life is more complicated than any single study.

The live fast, die young approach that is motivated by an uncertain future leads to shortsighted decisions, from payday loans to selling drugs to dropping out of school, that provide short-term rewards but sabotage the future. It also encourages young people to have children sooner and discourages marriage, the biggest long-term commitment that most people ever make. This lack of a stable family life also sabotages their children's future. The emergency response of our stress and immune systems to daily crises gives us the energy to get us out of those scrapes, but at the expense of sabotaging our future well-being. The feelings of insecurity cued by poverty, together with easy us-versus-them divisions fostered by inequality, provoke us to embrace simplistic beliefs, extreme ideologies, and prejudices that provide easy answers, but do so by sabotaging the healthy functioning of civil society.

Each of these factors can contribute to heightening the original insecurity and crisis state. Add to this dynamic the simple fact that people who can afford to move away from troubled areas tend to do so, leaving behind those with the worst problems and the least prospects concentrated in clusters of what sociologist William Julius Wilson calls the "truly disadvantaged." Individuals tend to make choices from the options that are familiar to them, taking pathways that are easy to navigate. A child born into such conditions is unlikely to know anyone who has escaped to college, or anyone who has ever been anything but poor. Those self-reinforcing factors create a kind of gravity that makes it increasingly difficult for anyone to escape them.

The gravity metaphor is apt, because breaking away from areas of concentrated disadvantage requires what I think of as an escape velocity. In physics, escape velocity is the speed required to escape a planet's gravitational pull. Once a projectile leaving Earth reaches that speed, it will keep going forever. When people escape an impoverished background, they, too, are gone forever in a sense. Even if they return, they think differently, speak differently, and even eat differently. A family member once told me she didn't want to set up education funds for her children because people came back from college as atheists. And what good is increased earnings potential when compared to eternal damnation?

In my own case, I was determined to escape, though I didn't fully realize the consequences that my doing so would have. Despite holiday visits, I will probably never again be as close to my siblings as those who stayed in Kentucky are to one another. My daughter will never know her grandparents with the same degree of intimacy as their grandchildren who live down the road. Living such different lives in such dissimilar places means that we share few assumptions about how the world works. Holiday dinners must be navigated between electrified fences of politics, religion, and current events. I and my family have undergone a predictable set of changes—predicted, in fact, by the scientific research presented in the previous chapters. There are good reasons why people with different experiences tend to have incompatible understandings of the world. But as the educated and wealthy pull further away from everyone else, those disparities are becoming enshrined in impermeable cultural barriers.

Understanding how inequality accelerates cycles of disadvantage can begin to help defuse many of the conflicts that arise when people discuss inequality. Take, for example, the ways one might explain the life of my uncle Sterman. Sterman lived in a barn at the county landfill. On winter nights when the temperature dipped close to zero, my father would go check on him and try to persuade him to come sleep at our house for the night. But he insisted on remaining where he was, hunkered down in a corner of the barn next to a coal stove. When I was little, I thought he was a black man because the soot from the coal—or the filth from the dump, or both—had so darkened his skin. My father once succeeded in convincing him to stay with us for a while, but he refused a room in the house. As a compromise, he took up residence in our barn instead. The space had been used years earlier as a pigsty, so my father built a floor over the dirt and covered it in red carpet. He installed electric lighting and hung wood paneling on the walls to approximate a home. My uncle resided there for only a few months, living, as far as I could tell, on Cheez Doodles and whiskey. Then one day he returned to his landfill.

If you want to interpret this account as an indictment of individual behavior, it is trivially easy to say that if my uncle had only stopped drinking, cleaned himself up, and gone back to work, he would have had a better life. It is obviously true that his choices contributed to a diminished existence. But that argument doesn't really explain anything, because it immediately begs the question, why would someone persist in behaving that way? Self-destructive behavior violates the basic assumptions of economics because it means turning away from a higher-value outcome in favor of a worse one. It is, from the perspective of an outside observer, irrational. To understand Sterman's choices, you have to know something about how the situation looked from his own perspective. You have to know what daily crises he faced. You have to know about his dreams, his disappointments, his losses, and his attempts to ease his heartaches. In other words, you have to know something about the damaging cycles in which he was caught. More than that, you have to confront the fact that we can predict with such accuracy that there will be many more Stermans living such lives in places with high levels of inequality.

When people debate between individual behavior like my uncle's and systemic factors as the source of inequality, as if the issue were an either-or debate, they are missing the point. Inequality affects our behavior, and differences in behavior can magnify inequality. While many who have studied the lives of the poor have recognized these self-reinforcing cycles between poverty and self-defeating actions, partisans on both the right and the left seem to immediately forget one half of the equation or the other as soon as they start proposing solutions.

Conservatives focus on individual agency and argue that we have to develop incentives to motivate the underclass to improve their lot. But the poor are driven by a more immediate and critical set of incentives. Their lives involve daily crises, which they attempt to cope with using the best short-term crisis management responses they have available. They have long since abandoned conforming to the economist's vision of rational responses to incentives and have replaced them with reactions aimed at keeping heads above water. Admonitions to start pulling up bootstraps ring hollow when you live in that world.

While partisans on the left recognize the importance of systemic factors like income inequality and inherited disadvantage, they too often minimize the role that individuals' decisions play in their fates. They are correct in contending that individual outcomes are partly responses to the environment and social structures, but their abstract system-level explanations would be more persuasive to most people if they acknowledged that the system's effects on any particular individual are reflected in the concrete choices he or she makes on a daily basis.

My uncle lived the rest of his short life in that junkyard barn. At the age of fifty-nine, after a lifetime of smoking and drinking and hard living, he learned he had advanced lung cancer. His last months were painful ones, because the doctors told him he could not take pain medicine and drink alcohol at the same time. He chose the whiskey. His choices, to a large degree, determined his fate.

There are those on either side of the political spectrum who view such persistent harmful behavior and conclude there's simply nothing that can be done to remedy it. It may indeed be difficult if not impossible to pull someone out of a self-destructive cycle once he is firmly entrenched in it. But throwing up our hands and declaring the situation hopeless is not only a moral evasion. It also ignores the fact that people's behaviors are responses to their environments, and those environments *can* be changed. Individuals make bad choices more often if they, like my uncle, grew up in a cabin with a dirt floor amid a family of coal miners and sharecroppers. They make those choices more often in a high-inequality country, like the United States, than a lower-inequality one, like Canada. Even the disparity between high-inequality states, like Kentucky, and low-inequality states, like Iowa, translates to significant differences in people's life outcomes.

The same forces that lead to vicious cycles among the poor also lead to virtuous cycles among the more affluent. If it seems obvious to you that it is better to sacrifice today for larger returns in the future, then you have probably been raised in an environment in which that kind of conscientious investment pays off. If you believe that most people can be trusted, you probably came of age in a world where most people were trustworthy. And if your stress response stabilizes once a stressful event is over, you are probably accustomed to being in a world that is essentially safe. If you have the good fortune to have these as your default settings, then you are being lifted in an upward spiral. Your future is likely to be bright, because in the modern economy your instincts are productive ones, aimed at long-term success rather than immediate crisis management.

When my daughter was about a year old, she discovered a game that was alarming to her parents. When she found herself on a bed or sofa, she would stumble to the edge, squeal with laughter, and fling herself off, fully confident in the knowledge that someone would be there to catch her. I suffered a lot of skinned knees and elbows to make those catches, but she never hit the ground. I knew that my intervention only encouraged the game, but I couldn't bring myself to let her learn the hard way that it was a dangerous game. In part it was because I worried that she might really hurt herself. But more than that, I wanted her to believe that she lived in a world where she could go out on a limb and someone would be there to catch her. It was one small way to nudge her cycle of expectations in the right direction.

Until recently, cycles of poverty were thought to be driven only by material scarcity. It has become increasingly clear that relative poverty and the inequality that drives it are just as important in separating the haves and have-nots. When I told my friends that I was writing a book about economic inequality, they shared their stories about growing up poor. When I informed my academic colleagues about the project, they sent me scientific articles about the effects of poverty on brains and bodies. No one offered accounts about the richest people in their towns, or articles discussing the salaries of baseball stars or bank executives. But inequality is driven as much by the wealth of the wealthy as by the poverty of the poor.

It is natural to focus on the poor when considering the effects of the great gap between the wealthy and the impoverished in contemporary societies. Asked why he robbed banks, the famous criminal Willie Sutton supposedly answered, "Because that's where the money is." If we asked humanitarians why they help the poor, they might likewise answer, "Because that's where the need is." Alleviating poverty is of course an essential goal for both moral and practical reasons. Poverty devastates every aspect of an individual's life. In developing nations, where poverty deprives people of basic human needs, it is clearly a higher priority than inequality. But in developed nations, poverty is largely relative. It's less an issue of having no clothes on your back than one of sending your children to school in clothes that fill them with shame because they're not the right label. Here, fighting poverty is critical, but it is only half the battle.

The necessity of seriously confronting inequality and not just material poverty suggests the startling conclusion that we cannot simply grow our way out of our current predicament. Just as people often confuse inequality with poverty, they often confuse the goal of reducing inequality with the goal of fostering economic growth. But the findings on the critical role played by inequality itself—on health, decision making, political and social divisions—argue that economic growth by itself is not sufficient. The inequality reflected in statistics like the Gini coefficient is driven almost entirely by how wealthy the rich are. If some economic genius were to come up with an innovation that doubled everyone's income overnight, it would make the problems of inequality worse, not better, as multiplying the income of millionaires would increase their wealth by a greater amount than doubling the income of someone earning $15,000 a year. Everyone would be wealthier, but inequality would grow that much more pronounced.

You can see this pattern at work in the way that people's happiness tracks with their income. Happiness can be used as an emotional barometer for how a person's life is going overall, as it measures many of the health, stress, and social indices we have focused on in these pages. Starting in the 1970s, economist Richard Easterlin found again and again that, within a given country, richer people were happier—but only up to a point. A massive study published in 2010 suggests that the turning point in America is around $75,000. Above that amount, the effect of money on emotional well-being levels off: Those making $80,000 a year are no less happy than those making $8 million.

As most people in our country make less than $75,000 (the median American household income in 2015 was about $54,000), one could logically conclude that greater economic growth should increase the average happiness. The surprising thing is, however, that it doesn't. People quickly adapt to their higher economic status, as each rise in income becomes the set point for the new normal. As a result, average happiness is entirely unrelated to economic growth over time. This surprising finding has become known as the Easterlin paradox.

By standard economic metrics, the last fifty years have been incredibly good to America. Our gross domestic product has risen year after year. If you look at GDP per person since the 1950s, you see a soaring straight-line increase. Even the painful financial crisis of 2008 and the recession that followed represent only a small dip in the line, and we have continued growing since then. If economic growth were all that mattered, then we would all be having the time of our lives. Yet as a nation we have rarely been more dissatisfied. I was recently on a plane from Raleigh to Boston when I overheard a conversation between two women in the seats behind me that captured the national mood perfectly. An older woman with a Boston accent remarked, "It's gone to shit. Everything's gone to shit. The economy is terrible. Crime is crazy—I mean, I just go to work and come home and I don't even go out." The younger woman, who had a Southern accent, sighed knowingly. "It makes you wonder if you want to bring a child into this world," she said. These were women who could afford airplane tickets. They were traveling between two affluent cities during a period of historically low crime rates in the richest nation during the wealthiest period of the history of the world. Clearly, it didn't feel that way.

The key to understanding the Easterlin paradox is that the growth has not been widely shared. Almost all of it has gone to the richest few percent, leaving the incomes of most people flat, as we learned in the introductory chapter. If happiness is shaped by relative status, and inequality makes everyone feel left behind, then we would expect that high levels of inequality would be a better predictor of unhappiness than GDP. That is exactly what a team of psychology researchers led by Shigehiro Oishi found when they examined fluctuations in happiness among Americans between 1972 and 2008. Household income was not linked to happiness. But when income inequality ticked up or down from year to year, unhappiness rose and fell with it.

The Oishi study discovered that the inequality-happiness link was strongest among the poor, but it also affected the middle class. In fact, it affected everyone except the wealthiest 20 percent. But how does something as abstract as income inequality become a factor in a person's day-to-day happiness? A specific set of beliefs linked inequality to happiness. In times when inequality was higher, people tended to believe that others could not be trusted and would try to take advantage of you if they could. That distrust, in turn, predicted unhappiness.

Economic growth is clearly preferable to economic stagnation. But growth that continues to flow only to the richest will exacerbate the problems of inequality. So what is to be done? Understanding what science has discovered about the cycles of inequality and our behavior in reaction to them points to two approaches to solutions that I believe we should pursue simultaneously. One concerns the social context, and the other our response to it. The first is to prioritize building a flatter ladder. The second is to get better at living amid its rungs.

Obviously, shortening the ladder—reducing inequality—is the most immediate and powerful way to approach the many problems that have been explored here, because it approaches many of them simultaneously. Traditionally, policy experts have focused on finding specific solutions to one issue at a time. Medical experts seek to improve health. Criminologists formulate policies to reduce crime. Education experts design ways to improve schools, and so on. There are surely unique aspects to each of the societal troubles we face. But so many of them have extreme economic inequality as a common denominator that it would be foolish not to try to confront it directly. Two of the most astonishingly effective public health accomplishments in human history were antibiotics and public sanitation (sewer systems and chlorinated water). These innovations saved millions of lives and dramatically lengthened life spans in the twentieth century. They didn't do so by killing a single bacterium or preventing only one disease at a time. They were so successful because they had an across-the-board effect on thousands of infectious diseases.

Reducing inequality, similarly, has the potential to address scores of problems at once. But that requires moving away from seeing inequality through a moralizing lens. Instead, I believe we have to view inequality as a public health problem.

In practical terms, reducing inequality means both raising the bottom rungs of the social ladder and lowering the top ones. Many books have discussed the virtues of various types of policies aimed at doing so. Some of these measures are favored by the left, such as raising the minimum wage, expanding early childhood education, capping executive pay, strengthening unions, and increasing paid parental leave. Other proposed solutions rely on market forces to reduce inequality, which may make them more attractive to conservatives and libertarians. For example, research led by Bhavya Mohan found that when customers learn that a corporation has high pay inequality between the CEO and regular workers, they are willing to penalize it by buying from a competitor with lower inequality.

Still other policies have more general nonpartisan support. For example, both liberals and conservatives have at times supported expanding the Earned Income Tax Credit, which subsidizes the income of poor working families. Liberals like it because it provides benefits to the poor, and conservatives like it because it rewards work. More dramatically, providing a guaranteed basic income has also been advocated by both progressives and libertarians. The appeal to libertarians is that it would be more efficient to provide money in a single payment rather than via dozens of separate government-administered programs.

I have at times encountered dismay in the classroom when I've argued that inequality is essentially a public health problem that requires solutions from both markets and governments. One day a student shouted, "But that's just socialism!" That response is a common one to any deviation from unregulated markets as a means of promoting greater equality. But the argument doesn't hold water. Advocating for reducing today's extreme levels of inequality is not advocating for a socialist system, any more than efforts to reduce binge drinking are a demand for prohibition or a call to reduce the speed limit is an effort to slow traffic to a crawl.

Some context is in order. We saw in Chapter 2 that a whole range of social problems, from teenage births to high school dropout rates to violent crime, are all higher in states with greater income inequality. We saw in Chapter 5 that greater equality was linked to longer lives when comparing countries, as well as when comparing across the states. These statistics suggest that reducing income inequality from the rates of Kentucky or Louisiana to the rates of Iowa or Utah could transform the lives of millions of people. Iowa is not a socialist paradise of the proletariat, but the lives and life expectancies of its citizens are measurably better than in states with higher levels of inequality.

The goal is not to eliminate all inequality, which, however idealistic, has never been a feasible model. Utopian ideals have a way of becoming dystopian realities. Rather, the goal is to adjust the level of inequality to a more human scale, one that gives people ample room to compete and to move up in their lives, without making economic competition a winner-take-all contest. A degree of inequality is a natural outcome of competition in a market economy, and in that system there will always be winners and losers. A number of people extrapolate from that basic point, however, to conclude that if some inequality is good for social mobility, then even higher inequality must be that much better.

That logic turns out to be exactly backward. Nations, states, and regions with higher degrees of income inequality actually have less upward mobility, a relationship known as the Gatsby curve. From a slightly different perspective, this means that the more inequality there is in the area in which you live, the more your economic prospects are determined by your parents' wealth rather than by your own success. When the rungs of the economic ladder are farther apart, it becomes that much more difficult to climb them.

Changing the fundamentals of the economic landscape is a long-term prospect, but there are other strategies suggested by the science of inequality that can improve the quality of individual lives on a more immediate basis. The first is to choose social comparisons wisely.

I argued earlier that social comparisons are an inevitable part of daily existence. Given that we compare ourselves to other people so promiscuously, and relative comparisons are so ingrained in the way we judge just about everything, how can we compare wisely if we are often not consciously aware that we are doing so?

The answer is that unconscious thoughts are not, as traditionally believed, walled off in some Freudian cave, impossible to access. Today psychologists consider most unconscious thinking to be of a different nature entirely. Reading is one good example. When you first learned how to decipher strings of letters into words, it was a slow and effortful process and required all your attention. But as you became more and more skilled, reading became effortless and automatic. You were no longer aware of sounding out syllables into words and connecting words to ideas, although that is exactly what your brain was doing. Or consider, as you are reading this sentence, that you are likely to be unaware of your breathing, or the amount of pressure on your gluteus maximus. We lose our awareness of what we are doing or feeling when the activity becomes so routine that we no longer need to pay attention. But that doesn't mean that we can't become conscious of it by voluntarily directing attention toward it. As with breathing, once we attend to it, we can often exert some control over what we are doing.

A cue that you are in the grips of unconscious social comparison is the vague anxiety that something you have isn't quite good enough. We think that there's something wrong with our laminate countertop because it's not granite, or that our granite is inferior because it's not marble. We make this sort of calculation constantly, with respect to possessions ranging from the homes we live in to the shoes we wear. In most cases, there is no true standard for what counts as "good enough." We are unconsciously comparing what we have to what someone else has—our friends, our neighbors, that handsome couple in the magazine—and we are aware only of the conclusion our brain has silently computed: Compared to that, this isn't sufficient.

That *discrepancy* is the signature of upward social comparisons. Most commonly, it is experienced in the world of objects around us rather than in our own heads. My countertop looks drab. My wardrobe looks dated. These objects themselves haven't changed, but our perception of them has. The sensation that there is something deficient in them has a doubly seductive quality: It not only motivates us to want more, but it also justifies these desires by providing physical evidence in support of that desire. Social comparison masquerading as "something's wrong with my stuff" is a major reason that so many people live paycheck to paycheck, even when they have a good income. Upward social comparison is a constant pressure nudging us to the outermost limits of what we can afford.

We can, in fact, exert more control over how we compare. Controlled comparison means, first, learning to recognize when we are in the grips of such a compulsion and, second, choosing wisely what kind of comparison is really relevant and useful. The idea here is not to stop comparing; it is to compare more wisely.

Different types of comparisons have different effects. Upward comparisons make us feel poorer, less talented, and needier. So if your goal is to manage those feelings and desires, redirect your attention to a downward comparison instead. Am I suggesting here that you should think about others who are less fortunate than you in order to feel better by comparison? Doesn't that seem mean-spirited and petty? Yes, I am, in fact, suggesting precisely that. Downward comparisons are not only the source of schadenfreude and smug pride; they can also be a source of gratitude. The key is to be aware that, under different circumstances or as the result of an unexpected change in fortune, you could have been less fortunate, too.

Upward and downward comparisons both involve trade-offs. The danger of downward comparisons is complacency: When you begin to feel better off than someone else, it becomes more tempting to apply less effort in your life. Upward comparisons, in contrast, can inspire us to work harder and achieve more, but they are legitimately motivating only if we believe that our targets are realistic. Comparing ourselves to the Albert Einsteins and Michael Jordans of the world just makes us feel miserable and demotivated.

Successfully negotiating a balance in comparisons requires being clear about your goals. For example, are you aspiring to further your education or establish yourself in your career? In such cases, selective upward comparisons might be beneficial—though not to others who are merely rich or successful, but to individuals who have excelled in your areas of interest. If, on the other hand, you are someone who has fulfilled or exceeded your basic needs yet still feel as if you never have quite enough, a downward comparison may provide a healthy recalibration.

My wife has a useful method of putting downward comparisons into practice. Whenever she catches herself complaining about something, her mind immediately goes to the worst-case scenario, and she feels grateful to have that "something" at all. If her feet hurt, for example, her next thought is: *But I'm thankful I have feet!* She is not feeling superior to the footless of the world, but instead reminding herself in a concrete way that feet are a blessing, and her situation could be worse.

The point is not to compare with the winners, or to compare with the losers. It is to compare, with lucidity. Deploying both upward and downward comparisons is a way of putting brackets around our experience. Those upper and lower limits provide a sensible framework and perspective, reminding us that, while our situation could be better, it could also be far worse. While context can allow you to be a little more at peace with the way things actually are, if you are facing a major challenge and need every bit of grit you can muster, by all means indulge in some upward comparisons.

Another option is to redirect your comparisons from other people to your own past. If you have overcome important challenges over the course of your life, then comparing your present to your former self has the advantages of comparing both upward and downward at the same time. You get the benefits of downward comparison ("At least I'm not my goofy teenage self!") and also acknowledging your upward trajectory ("Look out world, here I come!").

Because we habitually make social comparisons to the people we encounter in everyday contexts, another way to manage the effects of inequality is to change those contexts. So in addition to changing your comparisons, you can choose your situations wisely.

About four in ten Americans never leave the towns where they were born. Another 20 percent change towns but remain in their home state. The movers are most often motivated by better economic opportunity, and they tend to find it. They earn higher average incomes and attain higher levels of education than those who stay. Those who stay tend to rely more on their network of family and friends. Moving away from home or remaining both involve a series of compromises, and there is no right answer for everyone. If you have the means to move away from a high-poverty area, that is often a sensible thing to do. But those opportunities will come at the expense of abandoning familiar social norms and cultural values, and an extended family who can provide practical support at many levels.

Not all significant moves have to be away from family and friends, however. Even switching from one neighborhood to another in the same area can have profound effects. A massive randomized experiment by the U.S. Department of Housing and Urban Development revealed that moving a family from a high-poverty neighborhood caused significant changes in their lives. One group was randomly selected to receive a housing voucher that subsidized their rent to enable them to move; a control group also received a rent subsidy but without moving. The subsidy was not very large, so in reality the families moved from very poor neighborhoods to somewhat less poor ones. Nonetheless, the results were striking. The children of families that moved were less likely to become single parents and more likely to stay in school and to attend college. By the time they were in their midtwenties, they earned 31 percent more than those who had stayed in their old neighborhoods.

Similar effects were found in another study in which the city of Chicago decided to demolish some of its low-income housing projects. The city provided the buildings' residents with housing vouchers to move to areas with less concentrated poverty. Compared with tenants who lived in other housing projects, those who moved had better employment rates and earned higher salaries. In both studies, the benefits of moving were more pronounced for those who were children at the time of the move, suggesting that one of the major ways that mobility improves outcomes is by creating a stronger, more stable home that eventually benefits the next generation.

An alternative strategy to moving to a more affluent neighborhood is to relocate to an area that has a lower rate of inequality. Data on inequality for each state, county, and zip code are available from the U.S. Census Bureau website. A neighborhood with lower inequality can provide benefits for you and your children without higher living expenses or property values.

The strategies I've been discussing are aimed mainly at those individuals, either low income or middle class, who feel that they are struggling or being left behind. But the issues are different if you are in the top 20 percent or so of the income ladder. Economically, the rising inequality of recent decades is likely to be good for you. And yet recent studies suggest that high inequality has some disadvantages that may be less obvious than one's net worth.

First, we have seen evidence that high inequality is associated with higher rates of crime, greater risk of stress-related illness, and greater political polarization. These problems degrade the quality of life for everyone, including the affluent. This may be why people are happier in more equal places even after adjusting for their individual incomes.

A second reason that the wealthy should care about reducing inequality has less to do with tangible outcomes and more to do with the kind of person you become. Many people believe that once they make their fortune, they will stop striving, stop comparing, and be satisfied with their success. Few remain satisfied for long, however, and high-inequality contexts make contentment even harder. One study compared each state's level of inequality with the most frequent Google searches in each state. It found that the strongest correlate of inequality was searches for luxury goods. The higher the inequality in a person's state, the more they seek to display their wealth with flashy jewelry, cars, and accessories. Many studies have found, however, that spending money on luxury goods does not increase well-being. For the affluent, higher levels of inequality tend to accelerate the social comparison treadmill, in which you have to run faster to stay in place.

Higher levels of inequality also encourage immodesty among the successful in other ways. Recall that our studies of the stock-picking game, as well as Lerner's studies that randomized subjects to success or failure, both found that when people succeeded at something, they immediately took credit. Even when their accomplishment had been randomly determined by the experimenters, successful subjects assumed it was their own hard work and talent that entitled them to their rewards.

Studies led by psychologist Paul Piff suggest that this sense of entitlement has unfortunate consequences. In one study, the researchers observed cars at intersections, recording their make, model, and the condition of the car. They also noted how often the cars cut off pedestrians in a crosswalk or other drivers who legally had the right of way. The more expensive the car appeared to be, the more frequently the driver cut others off. In another study, the researchers left a bowl of candy in a waiting area and told participants that it was intended for children in another study. They found that subjects who rated themselves higher on the Status Ladder were more likely to eat the candy. Still another study found that people with higher incomes tend to give a smaller percentage of their income to charity, and this difference is magnified in states with higher income inequality.

When it is suggested to prosperous people that they may have had some advantages or privileges, their immediate response is usually to think, "I worked hard and I deserve my success!" Fair enough. Every successful person I know works hard, but they can also name multiple ways in which they benefited from good luck and the help of others. Economist Robert Frank has used computer simulations to examine the role of ability, effort, and chance in driving success. The computer simulation starts with the assumption that ability and effort together explain 98 percent of outcomes, and chance explains only 2 percent. Under those assumptions, most of the "winners" of the simulation generally have high ability and effort scores, as you would expect. But something counterintuitive happens as the "marketplace" of the simulation becomes more competitive. At the highest levels of competition, everyone has very high levels of ability and effort. At this elite level, what differentiates the very successful from the moderately successful is chance.

This is not to argue that the affluent are undeserving of their incomes. Performance in real life depends on ability, effort, and chance. But, as the simulation highlights, the higher up the ladder you go, the more your success is influenced by chance in addition to your abilities and effort. Reminding ourselves of our good fortune and dumb luck is a powerful way to combat the sense of entitlement that so often comes with success. It also helps offset the unreflective assumptions that the world is always a fair place where good outcomes await the virtuous and bad outcomes signal vice. Just as I suggested that pairing upward comparisons with downward comparisons can provide useful context, so can pairing our natural tendency to focus on our merit with a focus on our luck. The next time you find yourself thinking about how you worked hard and deserve what you have earned, ask yourself what lucky breaks you had along the way.

If you are successful and affluent, then you are in a privileged position to make a difference. You have more money to contribute, be it to charity or to political causes that advance equality. If you are an employer, you have the ability to set pay scales in a way that encourages rather than discourages collaborative work. Some entrepreneurs are already trying it.

Dan Price, the CEO of a credit card servicing company, read about the research I described earlier revealing that greater income improves well-being up to a point and then the benefits of additional pay level off. Based on that research, he decided in 2015 to increase the minimum salary at his company to $70,000. To make the plan work, he reduced his own salary from more than $1 million to $70,000 as well. Attesting to the importance of relative status, two upper-level executives quit because, even though their salaries were not reduced, they thought it was unfair to pay entry-level employees that much. But many more of his employees stayed. The reduced turnover is likely to save the company money on hiring and training new employees. And Price is betting that improved employee morale and loyalty will lead to higher productivity. Time will tell if this experiment is a success, but so far the business is booming. Employees were so grateful they recently pooled donations to buy Price a Tesla.

The final strategy I want to highlight applies to both the struggling and the prosperous. It seems, on its surface, to have nothing to do with social comparisons, income distributions, or neighborhood contexts. It concerns, rather, assessing what is most meaningful to you. I mentioned at the beginning of the book that when I ask people to write down the values and motives that matter most to them, the same handful of values come up again and again, and no one ever replies that they crave status.

Take a moment to think about a value that you cherish. You will likely come up with one that you have in common with nearly everyone else. You will probably focus on one that is personal, that connects you to loved ones or an idea larger than yourself. It will probably have little to do with climbing a social ladder.

Studies show that this simple exercise of focusing on what matters most can have remarkable effects on experiences of inequality. First, it makes people care less about what others think of them. In one experiment, college students were asked to take a few minutes to write about a value that was personally important to them. After choosing an item from a list of values and qualities (like relationships with friends and family, artistic skills, creativity, and so on), they were then asked to write several paragraphs about why this value was important to them and to describe a time when it played an important role in their life. Participants in a control group wrote about a value that other people might care about but that was not personally significant to them. Next, participants indicated how much they were willing to pay for a luxury-brand watch and for a non-luxury-brand watch. The group that wrote about a personally essential value cared less about the luxury brand than the control group. In another study, subjects who spent a few minutes writing about a key value showed reduced physiological stress when being evaluated by other people.

Psychologists Brandon Schmeichel and Kathleen Vohs found that spending a few minutes writing about cherished values also made people less impulsive and more likely to delay immediate gratification for longer-term benefits. These studies suggest that the live fast, die young mind-set cued by inequality can be mitigated by recentering attention on what one really cares about.

In the most ambitious values-focus studies yet, psychologist Geoffrey Cohen and colleagues harnessed the power of values to combat the achievement gap between black and white students. They created an intervention consisting of several short writing exercises that were administered during the course of a school year. In the experimental group, each writing assignment involved writing about a personally important value. Students in the control group also completed the writing exercises but wrote about values that were important to other people. When researchers examined the students' grade point averages at the end of the year, there was a substantial gap between the GPAs of the black and white students in the control group, but that gap was reduced by 40 percent in the important-values group.

That finding was not an anomaly. The team repeated the experiment with another set of classrooms and had the same results. When the researchers returned two years later, the values students had maintained their improved performance into the ninth grade. Another study led by Cohen and psychologist David Sherman found a similar reduction in the achievement gap between white students and low-income Latino students that lasted throughout a three-year follow-up period.

In another variation on this theme, psychologist Crystal Hall visited an inner-city soup kitchen in New Jersey and talked to people getting their meals there. She asked one group of participants to speak for a few minutes about an experience that made them feel successful and proud. She asked a control group to describe their daily routine. Hall then offered both groups the opportunity to complete forms to sign up for social welfare benefits for which they were eligible. A persistent problem in providing benefits to the poor is that many do not enroll in benefits programs that would help them simply because the process seems too difficult or confusing. Although they may know it is in their long-term interest, people are often too overwhelmed to do anything about it—another instance of short-term thinking and poverty feeding upon themselves. The study found that talking for five minutes about an empowering experience significantly increased willingness to enroll in benefits programs.

These surprisingly effective interventions didn't require millions of dollars in funding, decoding the human genome, or unraveling the mysteries of the brain. They involved only a few minutes of sustained attention, itself a precious resource, and a simple shift in perspective, from a standard economic model, in which people always respond rationally to incentives, to a more realistic psychological one. In this model, people habitually measure their relative position against their social contexts in order to judge their own worth. Making the conscious effort to consider what genuinely matters interrupts the unconscious default pattern of looking to others to gauge how much we value ourselves.

The developing new science of inequality has already shed much light on why human nature is so deeply interwoven with the Status Ladder. It is human nature, not economic theory, that links the private jets of the wealthy to the junkyard barns of the destitute, and to the rest of us in between. It is human nature that links affluent people contemplating the value of a Rolex watch to fourth graders standing in lunch lines with no money in their pockets. For creatures like us, thriving amid inequality ultimately means reshaping the ladder. Until then, understanding the behavioral science of inequality can help us live more gracefully in this vertical world.

ACKNOWLEDGMENTS

This book became real when my wife, Elizabeth Marsh, told me to stop being so abstract and just write about inequality as I have known it. I owe her thanks, not only for that wisdom, but also for thoughtful comments on chapters and for picking up the slack on my many "writing days." My family is present throughout these pages, and I am especially grateful to my brother Jason and my parents, Paula and Mitchell, who graciously let me tell stories about them the way I remembered them. All of the inequality research of which I have been a part depends on the hard work and intellect of my students and former students, especially Jazmin Brown-Iannuzzi, Heidi Vuletich, Kristjen Lundberg, Erin Cooley, Daryl Cameron, Kent Lee, and Jason Hannay. I owe thanks to my colleague Sam Fillenbaum for reading chapters and for countless conversations about science, books, and life. My formidable agent, Richard Pine, took my vague attempt at a book proposal and had the enthusiasm and persistence to help turn it into the real thing. And my marvelous editor, Rick Kot, provided a steady eye and hand that made the book better on every page. Thanks also to Mitch Prinstein for comparing notes and commiserating on the ups and downs of writing a first book. I guess we did it.

NOTES

Introduction

1 **Sharkey stood up on that flight:** "Virginia Man Arrested at Jacksonville Airport for Assault on Flight Crew," Department of Justice, U.S. Attorney's Office, Middle District of Florida, February 1, 2016, www.justice.gov/usao-mdfl/pr/virginia-man-arrested-jacksonville-airport-assault-flight-crew.

1 **Ivana Trump was on a flight:** D. Garner, "Socialite Ivana Trump Kicked Off an Airliner After Foul-Mouthed Tirade at Noisy Children," *Daily Mail*, December 28, 2009, www.dailymail.co.uk/tvshowbiz/article-1238731/Ivana-Trump-flies-rage-cabin-crew-unruly-children-board-plane-say-police.html.

2 **recent study led by psychologists:** K. A. DeCelles and M. I. Norton, "Physical and Situational Inequality on Airplanes Predicts Air Rage," *Proceedings of the National Academy of Sciences* 113 (2006): 5588–91.

4 **richest eighty-five people in the world:** "Working for the Few," Oxfam International, January 20, 2014, www.oxfam.org/sites/www.oxfam.org/files/bp-working-for-few-political-capture-economic-inequality-200114-summ-en.pdf.

5 **number of ridges in a fingerprint:** Francis Galton, *Fingerprint Directories* (London and New York: Macmillan, 1895).

5 **chemical properties of the ingredients in a Guinness:** S. T. Ziliak, "Guinnessometrics: The Economic Foundation of 'Student's t,'" *Journal of Economic Perspectives* 22 (2008): 199–216. The "bell curve" is usually used to refer to the normal distribution, but the brewer William Gosset discovered its close cousin the t-distribution by sampling Guinness. Both are generally bell shaped.

5 **chest circumference of Scottish soldiers:** S. Stahl, "The Evolution of the Normal Distribution," *Mathematics Magazine* 79 (2006): 96–113.

5 **Pew Research Center recently asked Americans:** R. Morin and S. Motel, "A Third of Americans Now Say They Are in the Lower Classes," Pew Research Center, September 10, 2012, www.pewsocialtrends.org /2012/09/10/a-third-of-americans-now-say-they-are-in-the-lower -classes/. Eighty-nine percent said they were either "lower-middle, middle, or upper-middle" class.

5 **distribution in Figure 1:** For other ways to make abstract economic ideas more concrete, see http://visualizingeconomics.com/.

7 **Figure 2 shows:** Data from C. DeNavas-Walt and B. D. Proctor, "Income and Poverty in the United States: 2013," Current Population Reports, U.S. Census Bureau, www.census.gov/content/dam/Census/library/publica tions/2014/demo/p60-249.pdf.

8 **under thirty said the American dream was dead:** "Survey of Young Americans' Attitudes Toward Politics and Public Service, 28th Edition," October 30–November 9, 2015, Harvard University Institute of Politics, http://iop.harvard.edu/sites/default/files_new/pictures/151208_Har vard_IOP_Fall_2015_Topline.pdf.

10 **cannot afford $400 cash for an emergency:** "Report on the Economic Well-Being of U.S. Households in 2014," Board of Governors of the Federal Reserve System, May 2015, www.federalreserve.gov/econresdata /2014-report-economic-well-being-us-households-201505.pdf.

Chapter 1: Lunch Lady Economics

13 **surprisingly small relationship between traditional markers:** N. E. Adler, E. S. Epel, G. Castellazzo, and J. R. Ickovics, "Relationship of Subjective and Objective Social Status with Psychological and Physiological Functioning: Preliminary Data in Healthy, White Women," *Health Psychology* 19 (2009): 586–92.

13 **If you place yourself on a lower rung:** The health correlates of subjective status are described in more detail in Chapter 5. Decision making is discussed in Chapter 3; work performance is discussed in Chapter 8; and conspiracy theories and other beliefs in Chapter 4.

16 **Lake Wobegon effect:** M. D. Alicke and O. Govorun, "The Better-Than-Average Effect," in *The Self in Social Judgment*, M. D. Alicke, D. A. Dunning, and J. I. Kreuger (eds.) (New York: Psychology Press, 2005).

16 **1965 study of accident survivors:** C. E. Preston and S. Harris, "Psychology of Drivers in Traffic Accidents," *Journal of Applied Psychology* 49 (1965): 284–88.

17 **massive survey by the College Board:** Student Descriptive Questionnaire 1976–1977, College Board, Educational Testing Service, Princeton, NJ.

17 **Sedikides and colleagues asked a group:** C. Sedikides, R. Meek, M. D. Alicke, and S. Taylor, "Behind Bars but Above the Bar: Prisoners

Consider Themselves More Prosocial Than Non-Prisoners," *British Journal of Social Psychology* 53 (2014): 396–403.

17 **college professors were asked to rate:** K. P. Cross, "Not Can, but Will College Teaching Be Improved?," *New Directions for Higher Education* (1977): 1–15.

18 **Most people rate themselves as more objective:** E. Pronin, D. Y. Lin, and L. Ross, "The Bias Blind Spot: Perceptions of Bias in Self Versus Others," *Personality and Social Psychology Bulletin* 28 (2002): 369–81.

18 **monkeys were given the option to look:** R. O. Deaner, A. V. Khera, and M. L. Platt, "Monkeys Pay Per View: Adaptive Valuation of Social Images by Rhesus Macaques," *Current Biology* 15 (2005): 543–48.

19 **humans and macaques share about 93 percent:** R. A. Gibbs et al., "Evolutionary and Biomedical Insights from the Rhesus Macaque Genome," *Science* 316 (2007): 222–34.

19 **Archaeologists tell us:** C. Boehm, *Hierarchy in the Forest: The Evolution of Egalitarian Behavior* (Cambridge, MA: Harvard University Press, 2009).

20 **Brosnan designed a simple exchange game:** S. F. Brosnan and F. B. De Waal, "Monkeys Reject Unequal Pay," *Nature* 425 (2003): 297–99.

24 **son of William Lee Rawls:** T. W. M. Pogge, *John Rawls: His Life and Theory of Justice*, M. Kosch, trans. (New York: Oxford University Press, 2007).

25 **Rawls's theory of justice:** J. Rawls, *A Theory of Justice* (Cambridge, MA: Harvard University Press, 1971; revised edition, 1999).

26 **step further to apply it to actual data:** M. I. Norton and D. Ariely, "Building a Better America—One Wealth Quintile at a Time," *Perspectives on Psychological Science* 6 (2011): 9–12.

28 **half of all pregnancies, and 80 percent of teenage:** "Trends in Teen Pregnancy and Childbearing," June 2, 2016, U.S. Department of Health and Human Services, www.hhs.gov/ash/oah/adolescent-health-topics /reproductive-health/teen-pregnancy/trends.html.

28 **about 25 percent of married people admit:** A. J. Blow and K. Hartnett, "Infidelity in Committed Relationships II: A Substantive Review," *Journal of Marital and Family Therapy* 31 (2005): 217–33.

Chapter 2: Relatively Easy

31 **Mollie Orshansky never intended to draw:** G. M. Fisher, "Mollie Orshansky: Author of the Poverty Thresholds," *AMSTAT News*, September 15–18, 2008; G. M. Fisher, "The Development and History of the Poverty Thresholds," *Social Security Bulletin* 55 (1992): 3–14.

33 **2013 Gallup poll asked Americans:** L. Saad, "Americans Say Family of Four Needs Nearly $60K to 'Get By,'" Gallup, May 17, 2013, www.gal lup.com/poll/162587/americans-say-family-four-needs-nearly-60k .aspx.

33 **among American households below the federal poverty line:**
   J. Siebens, "Extended Measures of Well-Being: Living Conditions in the
   United States: 2011," U.S. Census Bureau, September 2013, www.cen
   sus.gov/prod/2013pubs/p70-136.pdf.

34 **Adam Smith made this very point:** Adam Smith, *An Inquiry into the
   Nature and Causes of the Wealth of Nations* (London: Methuen, 1776).

36 **His team rigged some soup bowls:** B. Wansink, J. E. Painter, and
   J. North, "Bottomless Bowls: Why Visual Cues of Portion Size May Influence Intake," *Obesity Research* 13 (2005): 93–100.

37 **he conducted an experiment that appeared:** D. R. Brown, "Stimulus-
   Similarity and the Anchoring of Subjective Scales," *American Journal of
   Psychology* 66 (1953): 199–214.

40 **tested how accurately adults can judge social class:** M. W. Kraus
   and D. Keltner, "Signs of Socioeconomic Status: A Thin-Slicing Approach," *Psychological Science* 20 (2009): 99–106.

41 **Mussweiler asked whether this same social comparison effect:**
   T. Mussweiler, K. Rüter, and K. Epstude, "The Man Who Wasn't There:
   Subliminal Social Comparison Standards Influence Self-Evaluation,"
   Journal of Experimental Social Psychology 40 (2004): 689–96.

43 **link between electrical activity in the reward circuit:** J. Olds and
   P. Milner, "Positive Reinforcement Produced by Electrical Stimulation
   of Septal Area and Other Regions of Rat Brain," *Journal of Comparative
   and Physiological Psychology* 47 (1954): 419–27.

45 **reward network creates a kind of "common currency":** D. J. Levy
   and P. W. Glimcher, "The Root of All Value: A Neural Common Currency
   for Choice," *Current Opinion in Neurobiology* 22 (2012): 1027–38; G. Hol-
   stege et al., "Brain Activation During Human Male Ejaculation," *Journal
   of Neuroscience* 23 (2003): 9185–93; S. N. Haber and B. Knutson, "The Reward Circuit: Linking Primate Anatomy and Human Imaging," *Neuro-
   psychopharmacology* 35 (2010): 4–26.

45 **responds just as strongly to relative status:** K. Fliessbach et al., "Neural
   Responses to Advantageous and Disadvantageous Inequity," *Frontiers in
   Human Neuroscience* 6 (2012): 1–9.

46 **Why might people be less satisfied when they are paid more?:** A. E.
   Clark and A. J. Oswald, "Satisfaction and Comparison Income," *Journal
   of Public Economics* 61 (1996): 359–81.

48 **surveyed the vast medical literature on the relationship:** R. G.
   Wilkinson and K. E. Pickett, "Income Inequality and Population
   Health: A Review and Explanation of the Evidence," *Social Science and
   Medicine* 62 (2006): 1768–84. For an accessible overview of this re-
   search, see R. Wilkinson and K. Pickett, *The Spirit Level: Why Greater
   Equality Makes Societies Stronger* (New York: Bloomsbury, 2010).

Chapter 3: Poor Logic

58 **Venkatesh studied the economics of the drug trade:** S. A. Venkatesh, *Gang Leader for a Day: A Rogue Sociologist Takes to the Streets* (New York: Penguin, 2008).

61 **classic experiment led by psychologist Ned Jones:** E. E. Jones, "How Do People Perceive the Causes of Behavior?," *American Scientist* 64 (1976): 300–305.

61 **"fundamental attribution error":** L. Ross, "The Intuitive Psychologist and His Shortcomings: Distortions in the Attribution Process," *Advances in Experimental Social Psychology* 10 (1977): 173–220.

62 **Nature and nurture always work together:** R. Sapolsky, "A Gene for Nothing," *Discover* 18 (1997): 40–46.

67 **bred a population of about eight hundred fruit flies:** S. C. Stearns, M. Ackermann, M. Doebeli, and M. Kaiser, "Experimental Evolution of Aging, Growth, and Reproduction in Fruitflies," *Proceedings of the National Academy of Sciences* 97 (2000): 3309–13.

67 **Belsky and colleagues made an argument:** J. Belsky, L. Steinberg, and P. Draper, "Childhood Experience, Interpersonal Development, and Reproductive Strategy: An Evolutionary Theory of Socialization," *Child Development* 62 (1991): 647–70.

68 **Wilson and Daly looked at the average age:** M. Wilson and M. Daly, "Life Expectancy, Economic Inequality, Homicide, and Reproductive Timing in Chicago Neighbourhoods," *British Medical Journal* 314 (1997): 1271–74.

69 **By the mid-2000s, it was clear:** M. Del Giudice, S. W. Gangestad, and H. S. Kaplan, "Life History Theory and Evolutionary Psychology," in *The Handbook of Evolutionary Psychology*, D. M. Buss (ed.) (Hoboken, NJ: John Wiley and Sons, 2015).

70 **predicted that when people are made to feel poor:** M. J. Callan, N. W. Shead, and J. M. Olson, "Personal Relative Deprivation, Delay Discounting, and Gambling," *Journal of Personality and Social Psychology* 101 (2011): 955–73.

72– **Cartar was studying the feeding habits of wild bumblebees:** R. V.
73 Cartar, "A Test of Risk-Sensitive Foraging in Wild Bumble Bees," *Ecology* 72 (1991): 888–95.

75 **To test whether inequality actually increases risk taking:** B. K. Payne, J. L. Brown-Iannuzzi, and J. W. Hannay, "Inequality Increases Risk Taking," Working Paper, 2016.

78 **risky googling tracks real-life risky behavior:** B. K. Payne, J. L. Brown-Iannuzzi, and J. W. Hannay, "Income Inequality, Risk Taking, and Social Outcomes," Working Paper, 2016.

79 **Bradford, "There but for the grace of God":** E. Bickersteth, *A Treatise on Prayer: Designed to Assist in Its Devout Discharge: With a Few Forms of Prayer* (n.p.: A. Van Santvoord & M. Cole, 1822).

Chapter 4: The Right, the Left, and the Ladder

83 **Baron de Gauville:** M. Gauchet, "Right and Left," in *Realms of Memory: Rethinking the French Past*, P. Nora and L. D. Kritzman (eds.) (New York: Columbia University Press, 1997), 241–99.

85 **the left and the right consistently differ from each other:** J. T. Jost, C. M. Federico, and J. L. Napier, "Political Ideology: Its Structure, Functions, and Elective Affinities," *Annual Review of Psychology* 60 (2009): 307–37.

87 **No single bird knows where the flock is heading next:** H. Hildenbrandt, C. Carere, and C. K. Hemelrijk, "Self-Organized Aerial Displays of Thousands of Starlings: A Model," *Behavioral Ecology* 21 (2010): 1349–59.

87 **"Like a drunken fingerprint across the sky!":** R. Wilbur, "An Event," in *Collected Poems, 1943–2004* (Orlando, FL: Harcourt, 2004), 347.

89 **link between preferences for traditional power structures:** S. G. McFarland, V. S. Ageyev, and M. A. Abalakina-Paap, "Authoritarianism in the Former Soviet Union," *Journal of Personality and Social Psychology* 63 (1992): 1004–10.

90 **carry around an "ideological toolbox" in our heads:** A. C. Kay and R. P. Eibach, "The Ideological Toolbox: Ideologies as Tools of Motivated Social Cognition," in *The SAGE Handbook of Social Cognition*, S. Fiske and C. Macrae (eds.) (London: Sage, 2012), 495–515.

91 **show you the words "ocean" and "moon":** R. E. Nisbett and T. D. Wilson, "Telling More Than We Can Know: Verbal Reports on Mental Processes," *Psychological Review* 84 (1977): 231–59.

91 **what they call "choice blindness":** L. Hall et al., "How the Polls Can Be Both Spot On and Dead Wrong: Using Choice Blindness to Shift Political Attitudes and Voter Intentions," *PLOS ONE* 8 (2013): e60554.

94 **thinking about the role of individual merit:** C. J. Bryan et al., "Political Mindset: Effects of Schema Priming on Liberal-Conservative Political Positions," *Journal of Experimental Social Psychology* 45 (2009): 890–95.

94 **Bush's approval rating rose from 51 percent:** "Presidential Approval Ratings—George W. Bush," Gallup, www.gallup.com/poll/116500/presidential-approval-ratings-george-bush.aspx.

95 **the 9/11 group expressed greater support for President Bush:** A. J. Lambert et al., "Rally Effects, Threat, and Attitude Change: An Integrative Approach to Understanding the Role of Emotion," *Journal of Personality and Social Psychology* 98 (2010): 886–903.

96 **death group was more supportive of President Bush:** M. J. Landau et al., "Deliver Us from Evil: The Effects of Mortality Salience and Reminders of 9/11 on Support for President George W. Bush," *Personality and Social Psychology Bulletin* 30 (2004): 1136–50.

96 **whenever the terror alert increased:** R. Willer, "The Effects of Government-Issued Terror Warnings on Presidential Approval Ratings," *Current Research in Social Psychology* 10 (2004): 1–12.

98 **Thomas Frank's bestselling book:** T. Frank, *What's the Matter with Kansas? How Conservatives Won the Heart of America* (New York: Macmillan, 2007).

99 **"Nation's Poor Win Election for Nation's Rich":** "Nation's Poor Win Election for Nation's Rich," *The Onion*, November 10, 2004, www.theonion.com/article/nations-poor-win-election-for-nations-rich-1246.

100 **The richer you are, the more likely you are to call yourself a Republican:** A. Gelman, *Red State, Blue State, Rich State, Poor State: Why Americans Vote the Way They Do* (Princeton, NJ: Princeton University Press, 2009).

102 **consumer preferences of voters in each party:** "New Study Reveals That Democrats and Republicans Disagree on the Brands They Love Most," retrieved from buyology.com.

104 **people have almost no idea whether government programs:** S. Mettler, *The Submerged State: How Invisible Government Policies Undermine American Democracy* (Chicago: University of Chicago Press, 2011).

104 **"Homer Gets a Tax Cut":** L. M. Bartels, "Homer Gets a Tax Cut: Inequality and Public Policy in the American Mind," *Perspectives on Politics* 3 (2005): 15–31.

106 **Social comparisons led to differences in political beliefs:** J. L. Brown-Iannuzzi, K. B. Lundberg, A. C. Kay, and B. K. Payne, "Subjective Status Shapes Political Preferences," *Psychological Science* 26 (2015): 15–26.

108 **polarization that has split political elites:** C. Andris et al., "The Rise of Partisanship and Super-Cooperators in the U.S. House of Representatives," *PLOS ONE* 10 (2015): e0123507.

109 **As George Carlin put it:** G. Carlin, B. Carlin, and S. J. Santos, *Carlin on Campus* (MPI Home Video, 2001).

109 **You might be incompetent, you might be irrational:** R. J. Robinson, D. Keltner, A. Ward, and L. Ross, "Actual Versus Assumed Differences in Construal: 'Naive Realism' in Intergroup Perception and Conflict," *Journal of Personality and Social Psychology* 68 (1995): 404–17.

110 **subjects who thought they were:** J. L. Brown-Iannuzzi, K. B. Lundberg, and B. K. Payne, "Subjective Status Increases Naïve Realism," Working Paper, 2016.

110 **a measure of polarization based on how lawmakers:** N. McCarty, K. T. Poole, and H. Rosenthal, *Polarized America: The Dance of Ideology and Unequal Riches* (Cambridge, MA: MIT Press, 2016).

111 **Rutledge is a Republican who supported Arkansas's 2003 voter ID law:** M. Campbell, "Leslie Rutledge's Voter Registration Canceled; Candidacy Now in Doubt," Blue Hog Report, September 30, 2014, www .bluehogreport.com/2014/09/30/breaking-leslie-rutledges-voter -registration-canceled-candidacy-now-in-question/.

112 **threat to the nation's well-being:** "Political Polarization in the American Public," Pew Research Center, June 12, 2014, www.people-press .org/2014/06/12/political-polarization-in-the-american-public/.

Chapter 5: Long Lives and Tall Tombstones

114 **team roamed the graveyards of Glasgow:** G. D. Smith, D. Carroll, S. Rankin, and D. Rowan, "Socioeconomic Differentials in Mortality: Evidence from Glasgow Graveyards," *British Medical Journal* 305 (1992): 1554–57.

115 **life expectancy between rich and poor countries in Figure 5.1:** T. Jackson, "Prosperity Without Growth?: The Transition to a Sustainable Economy," Sustainable Development Commission, 2009, www.sd-com- mission.org.uk/data/files/publications/prosperity_without_growth _report.pdf.

115 **massive study of more than ten thousand British Civil Service employees:** M. Marmot, *Status Syndrome: How Social Standing Directly Affects Your Health and Life Expectancy* (London: Bloomsbury, 2004).

116 **the story "Silver Blaze," Sherlock Holmes:** A. Conan Doyle, "Silver Blaze," *Strand Magazine*, 1892.

117 **Status Ladder is a better predictor of health:** A. Singh-Manoux, N. E. Adler, and M. G. Marmot, "Subjective Social Status: Its Determinants and Its Association with Measures of Ill-Health in the Whitehall II Study," *Social Science & Medicine* 56 (2003): 1321–33.

118 **greater income equality had longer life expectancies:** R. Wilkin- son and K. Pickett, *The Spirit Level: Why Greater Equality Makes Societ- ies Stronger* (New York: Bloomsbury, 2010).

120– **death rate for middle-aged white Americans has been rising:** A.
21   Case and A. Deaton, "Rising Morbidity and Mortality in Midlife Among White Non-Hispanic Americans in the 21st Century," *Proceedings of the National Academy of Sciences* 112 (2015): 15078–83.

121 **Selye was a young Hungarian:** H. Selye, *The Stress of My Life: A Scientist's Memoirs* (New York/Toronto: Van Nostrand Reinhold, 1979); G. Gabriel,

"Hans Selye: The Discovery of Stress," April 5, 2013, http://brainconnec
tion.brainhq.com/2013/04/05/hans-selye-the-discovery-of-stress/. For an
accessible discussion of the stress response in humans, see R. M. Sapolsky,
Why Zebras Don't Get Ulcers (New York: Henry Holt, 2004, third edition).

128 **population in prehistoric times died a violent death:** L. H. Keeley,
War Before Civilization (Oxford: Oxford University Press, 1996).

128 **Sapolsky's work with baboons living wild:** R. M. Sapolsky, *A Primate's Memoir: A Neuroscientist's Unconventional Life Among the Baboons* (New York: Simon and Schuster, 2007).

129 **experimentally altered the hierarchy of monkeys:** R. C. Stavisky, M.
R. Adams, S. L. Watson, and J. R. Kaplan, "Dominance, Cortisol, and
Behavior in Small Groups of Female Cynomolgus Monkeys (*Macaca
fascicularis*)," *Hormones and Behavior* 39 (2001): 232–38.

130 **One study by Andrew Steptoe:** A. Steptoe, N. Owen, S. Kunz-Ebrecht,
and V. Mohamed-Ali, "Inflammatory Cytokines, Socioeconomic Status, and Acute Stress Responsivity," *Brain, Behavior, and Immunity* 16
(2002): 774–84.

131 **Muscatell and colleagues obtained similar results:** K. A. Muscatell
et al., "Neural Mechanisms Linking Social Status and Inflammatory
Responses to Social Stress," *Social Cognitive and Affective Neuroscience*
11 (2016): 915–22.

Chapter 6: God, Conspiracies, and the Language of the Angels

135 **Diane's grilled cheese sandwich:** "'Virgin Mary Grilled Cheese' Sells
for $28,000," Associated Press, November 23, 2004, www.nbcnews
.com/id/6511148/ns/us_news-weird_news/t/virgin-mary-grilled
-cheese-sells/#.WBTORtUrK70.

135 **Villagers in Russia:** T. Thornhill, "A Sign of Their Be-leaf: Christians
Begin Worshipping a Tree in Russia After Seeing the Face of Jesus on
Its Trunk," *Daily Mail*, October 2, 2014, www.dailymail.co.uk/news
/article-2777979/A-sign-leaf-Christians-begin-worshipping
-tree-Russia-seeing-face-Jesus-trunk.html.

135 **Christ in a smear of Marmite:** "Family See Jesus Image in Marmite,"
BBC, May 28, 2009, http://news.bbc.co.uk/2/hi/8071865.stm.

135 **Lord in his navel orange:** "Citrus Christ? Man Spots Jesus in an Orange," NBC News, January 12, 2010, www.nbcnews.com/video/nbcnews
.com/34823846#34823846.

135 **Holy Family has made appearances:** "Man Sells Mary, Jesus Funyuns
on eBay," *Charleston Gazette*, December 7, 2005.

135 **Hume noted in the eighteenth century:** D. Hume, *The Natural History
of Religion*, 1817.

139 **The Internet is full of discussions:** For example, "How to Win Powerball Prizes Consistently," www.lottery-winning.com/how-to-win-powerball/.

139 **Lustig, who has won lotteries seven times:** R. Lustig, *Learn How to Increase Your Chances of Winning the Lottery* (Bloomington, IN: Author-House, 2010).

140 **relationship between powerlessness and pareidolia:** J. A. Whitson and A. D. Galinsky, "Lacking Control Increases Illusory Pattern Perception," *Science* 322 (2008): 115–17.

140 **when people feel left out:** N. Epley, S. Akalis, A. Waytz, and J. T. Cacioppo, "Creating Social Connection Through Inferential Reproduction Loneliness and Perceived Agency in Gadgets, Gods, and Greyhounds," *Psychological Science* 19 (2008): 114–20.

141 **pollster asked more than 1,200 Americans:** "Democrats and Republicans Differ on Conspiracy Theory Beliefs," Public Policy Polling, April 2, 2013, www.publicpolicypolling.com/pdf/2011/PPP_Release_National_Conspiracy Theories_040213.pdf.

142 **about half of Americans believe in some form of conspiracy:** J. E. Uscinski and J. M. Parent, *American Conspiracy Theories* (New York: Oxford University Press, 2014).

143 **Lerner made this point by orchestrating an elaborate experiment:** M. J. Lerner and C. H. Simmons, "Observer's Reaction to the 'Innocent Victim': Compassion or Rejection?," *Journal of Personality and Social Psychology* 4 (1966): 203–10.

145 **Butler recently asked whether being highly paid:** J. V. Butler, "Inequality and Relative Ability Beliefs," *Economic Journal* 126 (2014): 907–48.

146 **"If God did not exist, it would be necessary to invent him":** Voltaire, "Épître à l'auteur du nouveau livre: *Des Trois Imposteurs*" (Letter to the Author of the *Three Imposters*), 1768.

146 **feeling powerless and insecure makes people more prone:** A. C. Kay, D. Gaucher, J. L. Napier, M. J. Callan, and K. Laurin, "God and the Government: Testing a Compensatory Control Mechanism for the Support of External Systems," *Journal of Personality and Social Psychology* 95 (2008): 18–35.

147 **a single "suffering index":** K. Gray and D. M. Wegner, "Blaming God for Our Pain: Human Suffering and the Divine Mind," *Personality and Social Psychology Review* 14 (2010): 7–16.

148 **Berger told the *New York Times*:** "A Bleak Outlook Is Seen for Religion," *New York Times*, April 25, 1968.

148 **about 84 percent of the world's 7 billion:** "The Global Religious Landscape," Pew Research Center, December 18, 2012, www.pewforum.org/2012/12/18/global-religious-landscape-exec/.

150 **Solt examined the level of religious belief:** F. Solt, P. Habel, and J. T. Grant, "Economic Inequality, Relative Power, and Religiosity," *Social Science Quarterly* 92 (2011): 447–65.

153 **Individuals who are religious tend to be happier:** C. H. Hackney and G. S. Sanders, "Religiosity and Mental Health: A Meta-Analysis of Recent Studies," *Journal for the Scientific Study of Religion* 42 (2003): 43–55.

Chapter 7: Inequality in Black and White

156 **since the first slave ship reached North America:** I. Berlin, *Many Thousands Gone: The First Two Centuries of Slavery in North America* (Cambridge, MA: Harvard University Press, 2009).

157 **Whites seemed to view discrimination as a zero-sum game:** M. I. Norton and S. R. Sommers, "Whites See Racism as a Zero-Sum Game That They Are Now Losing," *Perspectives on Psychological Science* 6 (2011): 215–18.

158 **racial gaps in wealth:** R. Kochhar and R. Fry, "Wealth Inequality Has Widened Along Racial, Ethnic Lines Since End of Great Recession," Pew Research Center, December 12, 2014, www.pewresearch.org/fact -tank/2014/12/12/racial-wealth-gaps-great-recession/.

159 **Pager tested for real-life discrimination:** D. Pager, *Marked: Race, Crime, and Finding Work in an Era of Mass Incarceration* (Chicago: University of Chicago Press, 2008).

159 **Kenneth and Mamie Clark:** K. B. Clark, *Prejudice and Your Child* (Middletown, CT: Wesleyan University Press, 1988).

161 **predicted by their appearance in their mug shots:** I. V. Blair, C. M. Judd, and K. M. Chapleau, "The Influence of Afrocentric Facial Features in Criminal Sentencing," *Psychological Science* 15 (2004): 674–79.

162 **imposition of the death sentence in Pennsylvania:** J. L. Eberhardt, P. G. Davies, V. J. Purdie-Vaughns, and S. L. Johnson, "Looking Deathworthy: Perceived Stereotypicality of Black Defendants Predicts Capital-Sentencing Outcomes," *Psychological Science* 17 (2006): 383–86.

162 **For Levar Jones:** M. Berman, "Former South Carolina Trooper Pleads Guilty to Shooting Unarmed Driver During Traffic Stop," *Washington Post*, March 14, 2016, www.washingtonpost.com/news/post-nation/wp/2016 /03/14/former-south-carolina-trooper-pleads-guilty-to-shooting -unarmed-driver-during-traffic-stop/?utm_term=.7354b90cf43d.

164 **one of the first experiments I conducted:** B. K. Payne, "Prejudice and Perception: The Role of Automatic and Controlled Processes in Misperceiving a Weapon," *Journal of Personality and Social Psychology* 81 (2001): 181–92.

169 **Feeling disadvantaged magnified their perception:** A. R. Krosch and D. M. Amodio, "Economic Scarcity Alters the Perception of Race," *Proceedings of the National Academy of Sciences* 111 (2014): 9079–84.

169 **bosses showed greater implicit racial bias:** A. Guinote, G. B. Willis, and C. Martellotta, "Social Power Increases Implicit Prejudice," *Journal of Experimental Social Psychology* 46 (2010): 299–307.

171 **The best predictor of wanting to slash funding:** M. Gilens, *Why Americans Hate Welfare: Race, Media, and the Politics of Antipoverty Policy* (Chicago: University of Chicago Press, 2009).

172 **Atwater described coded racial messages:** A. P. Lamis, *The Two-Party South* (New York: Oxford University Press, 1990).

172 **Ryan was accused of dog-whistling:** T. Kertscher, "In Context: Were Paul Ryan's Poverty Comments a 'Thinly Veiled Racial Attack'?," Politifact, March 14, 2014, www.politifact.com/wisconsin/article/2014/mar/14/context-paul-ryans-poverty-comments-racial-attack/.

173 **recently tested whether people really make this psychological leap:** J. L. Brown-Iannuzzi, R. Dotsch, E. Cooley, and B. K. Payne, "The Relationship Between Racialized Mental Representations of Welfare Recipients and Attitudes Toward Welfare," *Psychological Science*, in press.

175 **gulf between the views of white and black citizens:** R. P. Eibach and J. Ehrlinger, "'Keep Your Eyes on the Prize': Reference Points and Racial Differences in Assessing Progress Toward Equality," *Personality and Social Psychology Bulletin* 32 (2006): 66–77.

Chapter 8: The Corporate Ladder

177 **Ruiz dug graves for a living:** S. Terkel, *Working: People Talk About What They Do All Day and How They Feel About What They Do* (New York: New Press, 1974).

177 **people who do "dirty work":** B. E. Ashforth and G. E. Kreiner, "'How Can You Do It?': Dirty Work and the Challenge of Constructing a Positive Identity," *Academy of Management Review* 24 (1999): 413–34.

179 **Stouffer used survey research and statistical analysis:** T. F. Pettigrew, "Samuel Stouffer and Relative Deprivation," *Social Psychology Quarterly* 78 (2015): 7–24; J. W. Ryan, *Samuel Stouffer and the GI Survey: Sociologists and Soldiers During the Second World War* (Knoxville: University of Tennessee Press, 2013).

180 **In one classic study, groups of strangers:** P. E. Slater, "Role Differentiation in Small Groups," *American Sociological Review* 20 (1955): 300–310.

181 **scholars observed the daily routines of its employees:** R. I. Sutton and A. Hargadon, "Brainstorming Groups in Context: Effectiveness in a Product Design Firm," *Administrative Science Quarterly* 41 (1996): 685–718.

182 **plight of one CEO who had to drag himself:** L. Kwoh, "When the CEO Burns Out," *Wall Street Journal*, May 7, 2013, www.wsj.com/articles /SB10001424127887323687604578469124008524696#articleTabs %3Darticle.

182 **"Many CEOs have personal assistants":** K. Kneale, "Stress Management for the CEO," *Forbes*, April 17, 2009, www.forbes.com/2009/04/16 /ceo-network-management-leadership-stress.html.

182 **most direct evidence yet of the difference in stress:** G. D. Sherman et al., "Leadership Is Associated with Lower Levels of Stress," *Proceedings of the National Academy of Sciences* 109 (2012): 17903–07.

186 **University of California system:** D. Card, A. Mas, E. Moretti, and E. Saez, "Inequality at Work: The Effect of Peer Salaries on Job Satisfaction," *American Economic Review* 102 (2012): 2981–3003.

187 **wins and losses of every Major League Baseball team:** M. Bloom, "The Performance Effects of Pay Dispersion on Individuals and Organizations," *Academy of Management Journal* 42 (1999): 25–40.

187 **Similar effects were found in an NFL study:** M. Mondello and J. Maxcy, "The Impact of Salary Dispersion and Performance Bonuses in NFL Organizations," *Management Decision* 47 (2009): 110–23.

188 **golf, tournaments with greater inequality:** M. Melton and T. S. Zorn, "Risk Taking in Tournaments," *Managerial Finance* 26 (2000): 52–62.

188 **study of NASCAR racing revealed that greater inequality:** B. Becker and M. Huselid, "The Incentive Effects of Tournament Compensation Systems," *Administrative Science Quarterly* 37 (1992): 336–50.

189 **compared the quality of the products the companies produced:** D. M. Cowherd and D. I. Levine, "Product Quality and Pay Equity Between Lower-Level Employees and Top Management: An Investigation of Distributive Justice Theory," *Administrative Science Quarterly* 37 (1992): 302–20.

190 **interviewed by author Martin Sprouse:** M. Sprouse, *Sabotage in the American Workplace: Anecdotes of Dissatisfaction, Mischief and Revenge* (San Francisco: Pressure Drop Press, 1992).

191 **researchers persuaded the company to turn the painful pay cuts:** J. Greenberg, "Employee Theft as a Reaction to Underpayment Inequity: The Hidden Cost of Pay Cuts," *Journal of Applied Psychology* 75 (1990): 561–68.

193 **surveyed citizens from forty countries:** S. Kiatpongsan and M. I. Norton, "How Much (More) Should CEOs Make? A Universal Desire for More Equal Pay," *Perspectives on Psychological Science* 9 (2014): 587–93.

194 **only about 5 percent of the performance differences:** M. A. Fitza, "The Use of Variance Decomposition in the Investigation of CEO Effects: How Large Must the CEO Effect Be to Rule Out Chance?," *Strategic Management Journal* 35 (2014): 1839–52.

195 **soda drinkers cannot reliably distinguish Coke from Pepsi:** M. E. Woolfolk, W. Castellan, and C. I. Brooks, "Pepsi Versus Coke: Labels, Not

Tastes, Prevail," *Psychological Reports* 52 (1983): 185–86; S. M. McClure et al., "Neural Correlates of Behavioral Preference for Culturally Familiar Drinks," *Neuron* 44 (2004): 379–87.

195 **playing a Stradivarius or an ordinary violin:** D. J. Levitin, "Expert Violinists Can't Tell Old from New," *Proceedings of the National Academy of Sciences* 111 (2014): 7168–69.

195 **results of Fitza's analysis have been controversial:** T. J. Quigley and S. D. Graffin, "Reaffirming the CEO Effect Is Significant and Much Larger Than Chance: A Comment on Fitza (2014)," *Strategic Management Journal* (2016); M. A. Fitza, "How Much Do CEOs Really Matter? Reaffirming That the CEO Effect Is Mostly Due to Chance," *Strategic Management Journal* (2016).

196 **CEO pay is too high:** J. Jones, "Most Americans Favor Gov't. Action to Limit Executive Pay," Gallup Poll, June 16, 2009, www.gallup.com/poll /120872/americans-favor-gov-action-limit-executive-pay.aspx.

Chapter 9: The Art of Living Vertically

204 **effect of money on emotional well-being levels off:** D. Kahneman and A. Deaton, "High Income Improves Evaluation of Life but Not Emotional Well-Being," *Proceedings of the National Academy of Sciences* 107 (2010): 16489–93.

204 **the Easterlin paradox:** R. A. Easterlin, "Does Money Buy Happiness?," *Public Interest* 30 (1973): 3–10; R. A. Easterlin, L. A. McVey, M. Switek, O. Sawangfa, and J. S. Zweig, "The Happiness-Income Paradox Revisited," *Proceedings of the National Academy of Sciences* 107 (2010): 22463–68.

205 **period of historically low crime rates:** S. Pinker, *The Better Angels of Our Nature: Why Violence Has Declined* (New York: Viking, 2011).

205 **they examined fluctuations in happiness:** S. Oishi, S. Kesebir, and E. Diener, "Income Inequality and Happiness," *Psychological Science* 22 (2011): 1095–1100.

206 **antibiotics and public sanitation:** A. Ferriman, "*BMJ* Readers Choose the 'Sanitary Revolution' as Greatest Medical Advance Since 1840," *British Medical Journal* 334 (2007): 111.

207 **when customers learn a corporation has high pay inequality:** B. Mohan, M. I. Norton, and R. Deshpande, "Paying Up for Fair Pay: Consumers Prefer Firms with Lower CEO-to-Worker Pay Ratios," Harvard Business School Marketing Unit Working Paper (15-091), 2015.

207 **a guaranteed basic income has also been advocated:** N. Gordon, "The Conservative Case for a Guaranteed Basic Income," *The Atlantic*, August 6, 2014, www.theatlantic.com/politics/archive/2014/08/why-arent-refor-micons-pushing-a-guaranteed-basic-income/375600/.

208 **the Gatsby curve:** A. Krueger, "The Rise and Consequences of Inequality," presentation made to the Center for American Progress, January 12, 2012, www.americanprogress.org/events/2012/01/12/17181/the-rise-and -consequences-of-inequality.

208 **choose social comparisons wisely:** J. Suls, R. Martin, and L. Wheeler, "Social Comparison: Why, with Whom, and with What Effect?," *Current Directions in Psychological Science* 11 (2002): 159–63.

212 **four in ten Americans never leave the towns:** D. Cohn and R. Morin, "American Mobility: Who Moves? Who Stays Put? Where's Home?," Pew Research Center, December 17, 2008, www.pewsocialtrends.org /files/2010/10/Movers-and-Stayers.pdf.

212 **moving a family from a high-poverty neighborhood:** R. Chetty, N. Hendren, and L. F. Katz, "The Effects of Exposure to Better Neighborhoods on Children: New Evidence from the Moving to Opportunity Experiment," *American Economic Review* 106 (2016): 855–902.

213 **Chicago decided to demolish some:** J. E. Rosenbaum and S. DeLuca, "What Kinds of Neighborhoods Change Lives: The Chicago Gautreaux Housing Program and Recent Mobility Programs," *Indiana Law Review* 41 (2008): 653–62.

214 **strongest correlate of inequality was searches for luxury goods:** L. Walasek and G. D. Brown, "Income Inequality and Status Seeking: Searching for Positional Goods in Unequal US States," *Psychological Science* 26 (2015): 527–33.

214 **spending money on luxury goods does not increase well-being:** R. H. Frank, *Luxury Fever: Why Money Fails to Satisfy in an Era of Excess* (New York: Simon and Schuster, 2001); E. Dunn and M. Norton, *Happy Money: The Science of Happier Spending* (New York: Simon and Schuster, 2014).

214 **Studies by psychologist Paul Piff:** P. K. Piff, D. M. Stancato, S. Côté, R. Mendoza-Denton, and D. Keltner, "Higher Social Class Predicts Increased Unethical Behavior," *Proceedings of the National Academy of Sciences* 109 (2012): 4086–91.

215 **Frank has used computer simulations to examine the role:** R. H. Frank, *Success and Luck: Good Fortune and the Myth of Meritocracy* (Princeton, NJ: Princeton University Press, 2016).

216 **Price, the CEO of a credit card servicing company:** P. Davidson, "Does a $70,000 Minimum Wage Work?," *USA Today*, May 26, 2016, www.usatoday.com/story/money/2016/05/26/does-70000-minimum -wage-work/84913242/.

217 **focusing on what matters most can have remarkable effects:** N. Sivanathan and N. C. Pettit, "Protecting the Self Through Consumption: Status Goods as Affirmational Commodities," *Journal of Experimental Social Psychology* 46 (2010): 564–70.

217 **writing about cherished values also made people less impulsive:** B. J. Schmeichel and K. Vohs, "Self-Affirmation and Self-Control: Affirming Core Values Counteracts Ego Depletion," *Journal of Personality and Social Psychology* 96 (2009): 770.

218 **harnessed the power of values to combat the achievement gap:** G. M. Walton and G. L. Cohen, "A Brief Social-Belonging Intervention Improves Academic and Health Outcomes of Minority Students," *Science* 331 (2011): 1447–51; G. L. Cohen, J. Garcia, V. Purdie-Vaughns, N. Apfel, and P. Brzustoski, "Recursive Processes in Self-Affirmation: Intervening to Close the Minority Achievement Gap," *Science* 324 (2009): 400–403; D. K. Sherman et al., "Deflecting the Trajectory and Changing the Narrative: How Self-Affirmation Affects Academic Performance and Motivation Under Identity Threat," *Journal of Personality and Social Psychology* 104 (2013): 591–618; C. C. Hall, J. Zhao, and E. Shafir, "Self-Affirmation Among the Poor: Cognitive and Behavioral Implications," *Psychological Science* 25 (2014): 619–25.